A Collection of
"Nashville History Corner"

A Collection of

"Nashville History Corner"

Articles Written by Ridley Wills II
Between 2014 and 2022
for *The Contributor* Newspaper

ISBN: 978-0-578-28623-5

Editing: Amanda Varian
Cover and interior layouts: Lisa Parnell

Printed in the United States of America

This book is dedicated to
those formerly homeless men and women
who have, through grit and determination,
and by selling *The Contributor*,
found permanent housing for themselves.

Contents

Foreword

by Joseph L. "Jack" May

Whatever else distinguishes Nashville from its sister cities is that we alone have Ridley Wills II. His mammoth collection of published local history now exceeds twenty-eight deeply researched volumes. His writings are the steel strapping which bind the soul of the city—it defines us in ways that are palpable and permanent. It holds our past and directs its upward trajectory. Without Ridley defining our past, our future would surely be at risk.

The Wills family is our municipal treasure. As a group they have led the city in multiple diverse disciplines. A few through the generations would include insurance, law, medicine, poetry, publishing, history, and horse breeding among the many. Perhaps the most novel and effective is in the area of social improvement for the deprived. Tom Wills, Ridley's third son, has improved the lot of the community's homeless in meaningful ways with the brilliant innovation of *The Contributor*. It is a publication for deprived to buy and then to resell. The concept has given them an opportunity to participate in the commerce of our town and has moved hundreds of the homeless into warm, clean, and comfortable quarters. To *The Contributor* Ridley added a "Nashville History Corner," which is the underpinning for the volume at hand.

Did you know that a Nashville Harding was on the first round-the-world airplane flight? A few other notable questions of interest:

- Why did Belle Meade incorporate?
- Where is the Tree Trail?
- Why did Betsy Howe find it easier to live in a large house?
- Where is Richard Halliburton's dead body?
- Why is a West Nashville area called The Nations when the streets have state names?
- Was the Centennial Exhibition financed by government or private funds?
- What killed the Sedberry Hotel in McMinnville?
- What uniform did Nathan Bedford Forrest burn at Ft. Negley in 1869?

Ridley Wills has given us this bouillabaisse of potpourri—a most tasty dish for our enjoyment. So enter here and enjoy.

(Author's Note: Jack May, now ninety-two years old, is extremely bright and writes with skill and savvy. I sincerely appreciate his contribution writing the foreword to this book.)

Preface

Since 2014, I have written more than a hundred articles which have been published in *The Contributor*—the newspaper created in 2007 for the homeless and ex-homeless by my son, Tom Wills, Tasha French Lemley, Steven Samara, and Will Connelly. Now, fifteen years later, *The Contributor* is still sold on streets in Nashville by persevering men and women—many of whom are now living in subsidized public housing thanks to the money they are earning by selling the newspaper. To learn more about how *The Contributor* is changing lives, please visit https://www.thecontributor.org/.

Occasionally, I receive comments from people who enjoy my "Nashville History Corner" articles. In March 2021, a reader contacted my son, Tom, to tell him how much he enjoyed reading my article on Booker T. Washington and George Washington Carver. The article also included information about the Tuskegee Normal and Industrial School in Tuskegee, Alabama, where both men taught. At the conclusion of that article, I wrote that "at age eighty-six, I probably will never see Tuskegee" and commented that "I wished I had visited the school when I was younger." The kind man, whom I did not know, told Tom that he would be honored to drive me to Tuskegee for a visit. I called him and thanked him for his gracious offer, though I had to decline. Also read the "Hey Ridley" letter written by a *Contributor* vendor after she read my History Corner article #72 on my decision to leave American General.

In compiling my "Nashville History Corner" articles into a book, I have taken the liberty of correcting errors and mistakes, revising inappropriate or inaccurate titles, including new photographs, and actually rewriting certain articles.

Under the title of each "Nashville History Corner" article, you will see an issue date. These are the dates the articles appeared in *The Contributor.*

My final comment is that I will give the proceeds of the sales of this book to *The Contributor* in appreciation for what my son Tom has done for well over a decade—helping people get off the streets by selling the newspaper he cofounded and which he manages today with CEO Cathy Jennings.

Aerial View

Downtown Nashville 1959

The Contributor 7/20/2015

This aerial view of Nashville taken soon after the L&C Tower was completed in 1957 gives you a feel for the enormous growth Nashville has experienced since then. For a number of years following, the 30-story Life & Casualty Tower, designed by Edwin Keeble, completely dominated the Nashville skyline. The city's second tallest building then was the 15-story Trust Building completed in 1926 at the southeast corner of Third Avenue North and Union Street. Notice that below Broadway was an industrial area composed primarily of low-rise industrial buildings, warehouses, and parking lots. Only a small section of this area is visible in the aerial view. Equally as striking is the area immediately east of the river, where the Nashville Bridge Company had, in 1959, its boat and barge-building business on either side of the Shelby Street Bridge. To the right of the Bridge Company's office building, extending all the way to the Woodland Street Bridge was an industrial area. No Nashvillian in 1959 could have envisioned that today there would be an NFL stadium occupying much of that area!

Many early downtown high-rises, such as the 11-story National Life Building, the 12-story Andrew Jackson Hotel, the 12-story

Sudekum Building, and the 12-story Sam Davis Hotel were there in 1959, but today have been replaced by towers two and three times taller.

James Robertson Parkway, north of the Capitol, is not visible as it was not completed until 1966.

Nashville 1959   Courtesy of a local newspaper

Airports/Flights

Blackwood Field

The Contributor 9/15/2021

In 1921 the State of Tennessee leased 100 acres of pasture land on Shute's Lane adjacent to Andrew Jackson's Hermitage for use by the 105th Squadron of the Tennessee National Guard. The State brought two hangars from Memphis to Nashville and erected them on the field on Shute's Lane, which was named for H. O. Blackwood, a Nashville businessman who donated $1,000 of the $4,000 needed to build the air strip.

Aircraft flying in and out of Blackwood Field initially included Jennies and DH-4's, but soon these planes were replaced by O-11s, O-25s, and several types of private airplanes.

In 1924, the first north-south air mail flight landed and took off from Blackwood Field. The pilots were Lt. Vincent Meloy and Capt. Herbert Fox, a Nashvillian, who flew a DH-4 from Nashville to Chicago and back. Later, airmail service was expanded from Chicago to New Orleans. During all this airplane activity across the road, the ladies of the Ladies Hermitage Association, custodians of The Hermitage, became increasingly concerned that one of these "flying machines" would crash into President Jackson's home with dire consequences. Due to the pressure from these influential ladies as well as the need for a more centrally located airport, Blackwood Field was closed in 1928 and all activity moved to the city's new McConnell Field that opened in 1927.

Blackwood Field ca. 1924   Tennessee State Library

First Flight around the World

The Contributor 4/28/2021

Many Nashvillians know about John Harding, the founder of Belle Meade Stud horse farm; of General William Giles Harding, his son and successor at the plantation; and of William Hicks Jackson, the Confederate cavalry general, who married General Harding's daughter, Selene, after the war, and who ran the farm following his father-in-law's stroke in the early 1880s.

Few people know about John Harding, the son of John Harding III, who was called "Smiling Jack." He was one of a small group of army aviators who made the first flight around the world. At dawn April 6, 1924, four army single-engine biplanes named after cities took off from Sand Point Airfield near Seattle. One of the planes—the *Seattle*—became an early casualty when it crashed on the Alaskan coast. It took the crew ten days to reach civilization. A second plane, the *Boston*, came down in the North Atlantic while trying to reach Iceland.

Its crew were rescued by a navy cruiser. The crew members transferred to a new *Boston*, which came out from Nova Scotia and rejoined the two remaining planes for the final legs of the flight.

The three planes completed the vast circuit in the teeth of Canadian blizzards and Alaskan gales. While en route, Harding mailed a postcard to his old prep school headmaster, Sawney Webb. It read: "Mr. Webb, I'm not driving a quarter horse. I've got one that takes the same gait all the time."

From Alaska, the three Douglas biplanes flew over Japan, China, India, across Europe, England, Iceland, Greenland, and finally to Boston, where they were welcomed by President Calvin Coolidge. From Boston, they crossed the North American continent to the starting point, Seattle, which they reached September 28, 1924, having flown a distance of 26,345 miles in 371 hours flying time, averaging about 75 miles per hour.

Those making the flight were Lieutenants Lowell Smith, flight commander, and Leslie Arnold in the *Chicago*; Lieutenants Erik Nelson and John "Smiling Jack" Harding in the *New Orleans*; and Lieutenants Leigh Wade and Henry Ogden in the two *Bostons*.

Officers of the 105th Observation Squadron, Tennessee National Guard, welcome Lieutenant John Harding (center) to Nashville.
Photo by Barr-Hime Co., *Banner* staff photographers

Once the trip was completed, the young flyers were hailed as national heroes, and the six were given Distinguished Service Medals. John Harding was also presented with a chest of silver by the City of Nashville as an expression of pride in his share of the spectacular achievement. The presentation was made by Major E. B. Stahlman. Harding's feat was also acclaimed in a resolution adopted by the state legislature.

After his world flight, Harding went on a lecture tour with Lowell Thomas, and later founded an airline in Florida. He died in La Jolla, California, in 1968, forty-four years after his historic flight.

McConnell Field

The Contributor 9/21/2015

In 1927, the City of Nashville purchased 131 acres of farm land from Warren B. Sloan in West Nashville for a landing field site. The farm, nine blocks southeast of Charlotte Pike, was bounded on the south by the main line of the NC&StL Railroad to Memphis, on the west by Richland Creek, on the north by Colorado Avenue, and on the east by greenhouses on Westlawn Avenue.

On July 5, 1927, the city council voted to name the new field for Lt. Brower McConnell, a member of the 105th Squadron Tennessee National Guard, who was killed June 13 that year in a plane crash while flying maneuvers over Langley Field, Virginia.

Work on McConnell Field began later in 1927 when a dirt runway was leveled and two hangars moved there from Blackwood Field on Shute Lane. One hangar housed Louis Gasser's Nashville Flying Service while the other housed planes owned by Frank J. Miller.

By the following spring, fifteen sportsmen including the Gasser brothers, Albert and Monk; Frank Miller; Don Creighton; Guilford Dudley Jr.; Wesley Dyer; and Clay Jackson owned planes kept there.

Nashville's first regularly scheduled airmail service began December 1, 1928. Intermediary Interstate Airways pioneered the service,

McConnell Field hangar ca. 1928. Tritschler Nursery Greenhouses are behind the
hangar, and Murphy Road is to the left.   Courtesy of Metro Archives

flying a Fairchild FC-2W between Atlanta and Chicago with Nashville one of five intermediary stops. The plane that landed at McConnell Field at noon was named *Miss Chattanooga*. Within minutes,
it took off for Evansville. On board were two passengers and 7,500
airmail letters. At 2:15 that afternoon, the first southbound plane
from Chicago to Atlanta landed at McConnell Field where Governor Henry H. Horton spoke. After he finished, Miss Martha Lindsey,
former president of the Nashville Junior League, christened the plane
Miss Nashville.

On November 27, 1928, Evelyn Norton, of Joy Floral Company,
bought the first airline ticket ever sold in Nashville. Four days later,
she and William Howland, a *Tennessean* reporter, flew in a six-seat,
single-engine plane, also carrying a shipment of Joy Floral Company
flowers to Chicago. After taking off, the plane flew at an altitude of
1,000 feet all the way to Chicago.

McConnell Field serviced well the smaller airplanes of the 1920s,
including Taylor/Piper Cubs, Taylorcraft, Rearwins, Porterfields,

Waco 9 &10s, Travel Airs, American Eagles, Fairchild 4s and Ryans. Occasionally, Ford and Fokker Trimotors laned at McConnell Field.

Aviatrix Amelia Earhart visited Nashville in 1931. During her one-week stay, sponsored by Beechnut Chewing Gum, Miss Earhart demonstrated flying an autogyro and thrilled many local people by taking them in the air on joy rides.

In 1930, American Airlines began to replace their Fairchild FC-2s to Curtiss Condors and, subsequently, DC-2s, which McConnell Field was too small to handle. Recognizing this, American Airlines, with some assistance from the State of Tennessee, purchased in 1930 one-hundred eighty-eight acres of pastureland two miles southeast of Smyrna on U.S. Highway 70 for a new airport named Sky Harbor. The 105th Squadron Tennessee National Guard followed American from McConnell Field there. Nevertheless, McConnell remained as Nashville's official airport until 1938 when Berry Field opened on the east side of Murfreesboro Pike. Soon thereafter, the City of Nashville converted McConnell Field into McCabe Golf Course, which continues to operate there today.

Sky Harbor Has Nashville Flying High
The Contributor 3/9/2015

This flying field was located in Rutherford County on the north side of old U.S. Highway 70 South six miles northwest of Murfreesboro, Tennessee. On the day that the airport opened in 1930, U.S. 70 South was blocked for miles in both directions by automobiles, almost bumper to bumper, driven by people coming to witness the parachute jumps and loop-the-loop performances of Jimmy Doolittle and other skilled aviators.

Sky Harbor had a one-story, Spanish-style terminal building and single hangar. On opening day, visitors sat in chairs on the terminal roof, protected from the sun by colorful umbrellas, to watch the spectacle.

Sky Harbor remained Nashville's airport, with American Airlines the driving force, until 1938 when American and the Tennessee National Guard's 105th Observation Squadron moved to Nashville's new Berry Field, which opened on the Murfreesboro Pike about six miles from Nashville in June 1937.

Sky Harbor continued as an airport for a short time before most of the land was converted for use as a pasture for cattle, and the buildings converted to manufacturing uses.

Postcard views of Sky Harbor Airport and its rooftop seating area
Collection of Ridley Wills II

Front view of the James Robertson apartment-hotel building
Photo by Linda Bailey, *Contributor* staff

Apartments

The History
of James Robertson Apartments

The Contributor 1/5/2015

On January 23, 1929, a headline in the *Nashville Banner* read "Nashville's New Million Dollar Hotel." The article said that "Pritchett-Thomas Company would award a construction contract on February 6 for a $1 million, twelve-story apartment-hotel to be completed that fall at what is now 118 Seventh Avenue North. The new apartment, which will be the first built in the central business district since 1923, was initially scheduled to have 200 apartments, ranging from one- to five-room suites. Described as modern and fire-proof, the new apartment-hotel will include a basement garage and will compete the city's other large hotels—The Andrew Jackson, Hermitage, Noel, Maxwell House, Sam Davis, Tulane and Memorial Apartments."

The Sam Davis, which opened in 1928 on Seventh Avenue, one block north, and the James Robertson were sufficiently important to the city to justify new street lights being installed along Seventh Avenue North from Broadway north for two blocks. The James Robertson, which may soon be renovated, is currently an apartment building for low-income residents. The Sam Davis, on the northeast corner of Commerce Street and Seventh Avenue North, was demolished February 16, 1985.

Wellington Arms Apartments

The Contributor 3/3/2021

Wellington Arms Apartments, 4225 Harding Road, was one of the first high-rise apartments built in Nashville. When the seven-story building was completed in 1939, it was considered one of the strongest and best built residential buildings in the city. My grandmother, Elizabeth (Mrs. Matt G.) Buckner, lived there for a couple of years before her death February 15, 1947.

My wife, Irene Jackson Wills, sold Girl Scout cookies there when she was a student at Robertson Academy in the 1950s. Her grandmother, Irene Morgan (Mrs. William C.) Weaver lived there at the time as did several of Irene's elderly great-aunts. Nearly everyone living at Wellington Arms knew Irene and gladly bought a box of Girl Scout cookies, making it easy for her to be the leading Girl Scout cookie salesman at Robertson Academy for several years.

In the 1950s, Mr. and Mrs. Robert D. Stanford owned Wellington Arms. They sold the property, then in a park-like setting, for $1,350,000 to a group of Nashvillians, including Robert D. Short Jr., his son, Robert H. Short, and attorney Lewis H. Conner Jr. A few months later, the new owners converted the 52-unit complex into condominiums with leases of from six months to a year.

Quite a few years ago, the owners sold the land in front of the building along Harding Road, and shops and small stores were built. Upscale shops still are located there today. Although this change robbed Wellington Arms of its park-like setting, the condominium is still popular today with high ceilings and attractive rooms.

Baseball

Memories of the Nashville Vols

The Contributor 7/18/2016

In the summer of 1949, when I was fifteen years old, I was a huge fan of the Nashville Vols. Often with my best friend, Jimmy Meadows, I rode the city bus to historic Sulphur Dell on Saturday afternoons to watch the Vols, who were for many years the Chicago Cubs affiliate in the AA Southern League. That year, Manager Rollie Hemsley, who had just succeeded the legendary Larry Gilbert, led the Vols to the Southern Association championship and the Dixie Series championship by defeating Tulsa of the AA Texas League.

My favorite player in 1949 was Carl "Swish" Sawatski, who, during the season, had five grand slam home runs, and who led the Southern Association with 45 home runs, including a home run on opening day, April 15, that was considered the longest ever hit by a Vol player. It traveled at least 520 feet from home plate and was authenticated by *Banner* sportswriter, Fred Russell, who was in the press box. Sawatski went on to play in the major leagues and to be manager of the Arkansas Travelers and president of the Southern Association.

Nashville's star pitcher in 1949 was Pete Mallory who led the pitching rotation and ended the season with a 20–4 record and an ERA of 3.89. In the title run, he struck out 110 batters.

My favorite outfielder was Charlie "Bama" Ray. In 1949, his first of four with the Vols, his batting average was a personal best of .388 with

18 home runs. The power-hitting Vols' leading hitter in 1949 was Bob Borkowski, who led the league with a .376 batting average. Another big hitter on the 1949 team was Harold "Tookie" Gilbert, who led the Southern Association with 149 runs batted-in. He went on to play a portion of two seasons with Leo Durocher's New York Giants. He was a son of long-time Nashville Vol manager Larry Gilbert and younger brother of Charlie Gilbert, who played for the Vols in 1939, 1943, and 1948.

A final favorite, probably because he was a Nashvillian, was second baseman Harold "Buster" Boguskie, who played eight seasons for the Vols, beginning in 1947. Buster was the unofficial "Mayor of Sulphur Dell."

What wonderful memories I have of the Vols, and how I hated the Birmingham Barons, the Chattanooga Lookouts, and the Memphis Chicks.

Below: Teammates congratulate Carl Sawatski after a long home-run hit in 1949.
Nashville Banner

Businesses

Nashville Businessman Led Nineteenth-Century Telephone and Telegraph Co.

The Contributor 1/12/2015

In 1883, some Evansville, Indiana businessmen formed the Cumberland Telephone and Telegraph Company. One day, Nashville entrepreneur James E. Caldwell took part in a telephone conversation between employees in the telephone company's Nashville office and another group of employees in Evansville. Impressed, Caldwell later assembled a small group of investors and bought the company. Because he had other business interests, he initially took no active part in managing the telephone company. This changed when Cumberland Telephone floundered. Caldwell returned as president and CEO.

Under Caldwell's leadership, the Cumberland Telephone and Telegraph Company, whose headquarters he moved to Nashville in 1888, flourished, gaining control over telephone lines in Evansville, Louisville, Memphis, Nashville, and New Orleans. By 1910, the company had nearly 600 exchanges and more than 200,000 telephones.

Theodore N. Vail, the president of American Telephone & Telegraph, took notice of his rival in the South and acquired Cumberland Telephone and Telegraph in 1912.

The loss of Cumberland Telephone and Telegraph stung the pride of Nashvillians, many of whom had family members working for the

Home office of Cumberland Telephone and Telegraph Company
Collection of Ridley Wills II

company. Caldwell said "A great commercial tragedy has taken place. Nashville has lost its role as head of the Southern telephone."

Caldwell went on to merge Nashville's Fourth and First National Banks to become the South's largest national bank.

Harvey's Department Store

The Contributor 12/22/2014

In 1942, Fred Harvey moved to Nashville from Chicago, where he had been manager of the basement department for Marshall Field & Co. Here, he opened a new department store named Harvey's. Initially located at 514 Church Street, Harvey's merchandising and entertainment skills made his store a serious competitor to the city's established department stores. For example, in 1946, Harvey's installed the first escalator in Tennessee. His promotional innovations included a monkey bar and children's rides, the most popular of which was a merry-go-round. In 1953, Harvey's placed dozens of larger-than-life-sized Nativity scene figures on the east side of the Parthenon, facing West End. For fourteen years, Nashvillians came in droves to slowly pass by the white Nativity scene each Christmas to marvel at the display, which was bathed with white spotlights. The display was discontinued in 1967 because of the serious deterioration of the figures caused by the weather.

Collection of Grannis Photography

Above: Monkey Bar in Harvey's Department Store, downtown Nashville 1950s
Below: Until 1967 when he discontinued the annual display, store owner Fred Harvey had a Nativity scene set up on the east side of the Parthenon.

Nickajack Cave may have been named for an African-American man captured by Chickamauga native Americans at Clover Bottom.
Blueway, 2009, Wikimedia Commons

Cave

Nickajack Cave: Home to Bats and History

The Contributor 8/4/2021

Having spent much of the summers for nearly sixty years at the Monteagle Sunday School Assembly, it is hard to believe that, until the summer of 2021, I had never seen Nickajack Cave in nearby Marion County, Tennessee.

The cave is one of the most famous caverns in the state and likely has the largest entrance of any cave in the Eastern United States. The entrance is 140 feet wide and 50 feet high. To reach the cave from either east or west, turn off I-24 at the Kimball/South Pittsburg exit and drive the short distance south to South Pittsburg. Just as you enter the town, turn left and cross the Tennessee River on the spectacular bridge. Soon you will drive through the unincorporated town of New Hope, which some locals call "No Hope." You will see signs for the TVA's Nickajack Dam and Nickajack Cave, less than a mile upstream from the dam. At the cave parking area, you will see a sturdy wood walkway that will take you approximately 1/3 of a mile nearly to the cave entrance, which is under water from the dam on the Tennessee River.

Before Nickajack Dam was built, local people could drive automobiles to within a short distance of the cave. Today, there is a barrier across the cave entrance to keep people out. The top half of the entrance was, in 2021, open to allow bats to enter and depart from the cave.

While the cave entrance is in Marion County, its 3,500-foot length extends into Alabama and probably into Georgia.

Inside, a short distance from the entrance, the cave is nearly 200 feet wide with a mud floor. There are broken rocks on either side and a sizeable stream flows through the middle. In a short distance, Nickajack Cave narrows considerably as it extends southwest for 2,100 feet before reaching a large room 300 feet long, 90 feet high and 125 feet wide. There are many broken rocks in the room through which the stream flows.

Beyond the "Great Room," the cave forks. One branch, 325 feet long, extends into Jackson County, Alabama. It features several side branches mostly crawl spaces. The other fork follows the stream for 50 yards in a passage 5 feet wide and 8 feet high. This passage runs 850 feet to a so-called "Bat Room," a low chamber 50 feet wide and 90 feet long.

Beyond the Bat Room there is a crawlway 8 feet wide, 16 inches high, and 210 feet long. It leads to the final room in the cave, a chamber 35 feet high, 40 feet wide, and 100 feet long. In this chamber there is a huge flowstone formation, known as "Mr. Big." It is 60 feet high and 75 feet in diameter. At this point, it is generally thought that you are in Dade County, Georgia.

I became interested in Nickajack Cave because it was supposedly named for an African American slave, whom the Chickamauga Indians captured at Clover Bottom in Davidson County. At Clover Bottom, on the Stones River, Native Americans, in the fall of 1780, ambushed and killed a number of Cumberland River settlers, who included Donelsons and Gowers. These settlers had gone up the river in canoes to harvest some corn and cotton.

Native Americans used Nickajack Cave as a refuge. During the Civil War, it was mined by the Confederates for saltpeter and, for this reason, was shelled by Federal gunboats on the Tennessee River.

Churches/Synagogues

First Presbyterian Church (ca. 1920)

The Contributor 9/14/2015

This postcard view of the First Presbyterian Church was printed in about 1920. The church building, the third built by the congregation on this site, was designed by William Strickland, designer of the Tennessee State Capitol. Egyptian in style, the structure, dedicated Easter Sunday, 1851, is considered to be the finest example of Egyptian-Revival architecture in the United States. Notice the then-new Sunday School building behind the church. It was completed in 1918 and served for many years as the home of the Board of World Missions for the Presbyterian Church, U.S.

Someone walking up Church Street from Fourth Avenue in 1920 would see, in front of the church the sign "Christ Saves." Beyond the sign they would also

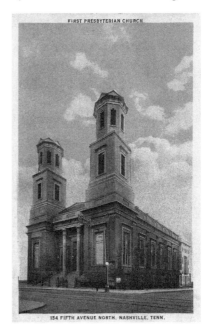

Collection of Ridley Wills II

21

see a sign for "Joseph Frank Clothes" which hung from the Jackson Building across Fifth Avenue North at Church Street. It appeared that the two signs were one that read "Christ Saves Joseph Frank Clothes."

In 1955, First Presbyterian Church moved to Franklin Road. A minority of the congregation chose to stay downtown and that year organized the Downtown Presbyterian Church, which is still there today serving the inner-city community. The Downtown Presbyterian Church is the home of the *The Contributor* newspaper, primarily founded in 2007 by Tasha French Lemley and Tom Wills. Tom's direct ancestor, Sarah (Mrs. Randal) McGavock, began worshiping on this site in 1818.

Downtown Presbyterian Church to Celebrate the 95th Waffle Shop

The Contributor 11/6/2019

The Waffle Shop began in about 1925 when the Women of the Church at First Presbyterian put on the event at the beginning of the Christmas season. Earlier called the Christmas Bazaar and Waffle Shop, it became a tradition at First Church and continued to be held annually through 1954, the last year that the church was located downtown on 5th Avenue North. Because the Downtown Presbyterian Church, founded in 1955, assumed responsibility for the historic downtown building, it also assumed responsibility for continuing the Waffle Shop, which benefits the homeless and the poor in the city's center.

One of the women at the Downtown Presbyterian Church who provided early leadership in putting on the Waffle Shop was Mary Thompson (Mrs. Sam) Orr. With her, Mary brought her cook, Katherine Douglas. Thirty-seven years later, in the early 1990s, when Katherine was eighty-four years old, and still cooking waffles, she reflected on the many years she had cooked waffles at the church. The recipe

In December 2014, Downtown Presbyterian Church members held their Waffle Shop. Volunteers cooking waffles were, left to right, Irene Wills, committee chairperson; Reverend Amos Wilson; Betsy Baylor; Susan Baughman; Betty McConnell; and Damaris Steele.   Collection of Irene J. Wills

that we still use was hers. Here it is: "For each batch, use two dozen eggs, a pound of flour mixed with a little salt and baking powder; a gallon of milk, and I have been using 2 1/2 cups of vegetable oil for the past three years and it works out beautifully." Katherine said the recipe makes more than fifty waffles. Avondale Rawls, who served as docent at Downtown Presbyterian for many years, described Katherine as "a fixture" at Downtown Presbyterian, and added that "she comes in on Monday and gets everything going and that's it."

In the 1960s, the Waffle Shop, traditionally held from 10 a.m. to 1:30 p.m. on the first Thursday in December, cost a customer $3. For that, you got one of Katherine's wonderful waffles and either sausage or turkey hash. Gradually, the price has increased to $10, and a couple of years ago we substituted hot chicken for the sausage or turkey hash. The crowd size has remained reasonably constant with 600 or 700 served annually with many regulars who have come annually for two decades.

For the past several years, Denny Harris and Mary Taylor have co-chaired Waffle Shop, which continues to be supported by members and clergy from First Presbyterian. The Waffle Shop has included baked goods, books. and crafts for sale.

[Editor's note: We were grateful for the community's long-standing support as we celebrated the 95th annual Waffle Shop on Thursday, December 5, 2019.]

A Look at St. John's Episcopal Church in Ashwood, Tennessee

The Contributor 11/11/2020

If someone asked me, a Presbyterian, what I think is the most beautiful church in Middle Tennessee, I would say that it's Saint John's Episcopal on State Highway 6 between Columbia and Mt. Pleasant. The church was the fulfillment of the dream of Leonidas Polk, the Episcopal Bishop of Louisiana and a major general in the Confederate Army. He gave the land, supervised the construction, and financially supported this three-year effort. His brothers, who owned adjoining plantations, also helped build the church. Enslaved people cut the trees and hewed the timbers for beams and floors. The foundation stones were quarried from a nearby site, and from a large wild cherry tree on the church grounds, the altar,

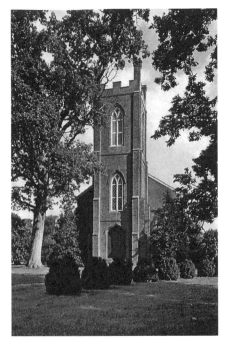

St. John's Episcopal Church, Ashwood, Tennessee
Collection of Ridley Wills II

communion rail, and balcony were made. Polk's mother gave the church a silver communion service.

The church building, which measures 42' by 65' and has walls sixteen inches wide, was completed in 1842 and the bell installed in the church tower in 1849. At the consecration service on September 4, 1842, White families took seats first and enslaved people, who built the building, and their families found places to sit where they could in the filled-to-capacity sanctuary.

Several members of the Polk family are buried in the cemetery behind the church. Also buried there is Bishop James H. Otey, founder of the Episcopal Church in Tennessee. Bishop Polk asked to be buried there. However, after he was killed on Pine Mountain near Marietta, Georgia, in 1864, he was buried in the crypt beneath the chancel of Saint Paul's Episcopal Church in Augusta, Georgia. In 1945, his remains were moved to Christ Church Cathedral in New Orleans because he had been Bishop of Louisiana.

Today, only a couple of worship services are held at Saint John's annually.

St. Patrick Catholic Church
Has Always Been a Servant Church

The Contributor 2/27/2019

This late nineteenth-century church was built about 1890 to serve Nashville's Irish community, then still strong in South Nashville. From 1892 until the 1960s, six itinerant Irish family clans—called by some, "gypsies" or "Irish Travelers"—came from all across the country the first Monday of May to hold an "Irish Wake" for their dead in St. Patrick Catholic Church, before the deceased were buried in Calvary Cemetery.

B. J. Hodge and M. Hodge, architects, designed the church at 1219 Second Avenue South. The building's architectural highlight is a pyramidal spire that tops a redbrick octagonal tower. St. Patrick Church is the city's "only extant ecclesiastical example of the Second Empire style." The building has a slate mansard roof, brick pilasters, and round-arched windows. In 1998, a fire damaged the building, but it was successfully restored. Since it was founded, St. Patrick has been a servant church. In addition to serving as a temporary home for a Catholic school, the church has also hosted civic and social club meetings, community picnics, and an annual St. Patrick's Day celebration. It has also housed the homeless.

One weekend in June 1984, my wife, Irene, and I went there as Presbyterian volunteers to help serve supper to the homeless. That evening, a young homeless woman asked Irene if she went to the Swan Ball held a week earlier. Irene, taken aback, said she did. The young woman then asked Irene if she met Picasso's daughter, Paloma Picasso, who brought a sparkling array of jewels from Tiffany's to sell at the ball. Irene, although stunned by the question, again said yes. Irene then learned from the young woman that she had attended Bennington College. After supper, Irene went home while I spent the night as one of several volunteers who did so. I remember that one family who spent the night there that evening as guests of the church had a family member who was to be executed by the State of Tennessee the next day.

Those who have experienced homelessness have stories and life experiences to tell if we can just take the time to serve them and listen.

St. Patrick Catholic Church still stands and serves on Second Avenue South in Nashville.
Photo by Don Morfe, courtesy of Metropolitan Historical Commission

Vine Street Temple

The Contributor 7/11/2016

The downtown space that is now occupied by the garage for the Nashville Public Library previously was occupied by one of Nashville's most striking buildings—the Vine Street Temple. From 1876 until 1955, the Temple was located near the corner of Seventh Avenue North and Commerce Street. The structure's nine Byzantine domes of various sizes always made me think of similar domes on buildings in Moscow. Built of pressed brick and cut stone on a 66' x 175' lot on the east side of what was then Vine Street, the building was originally surrounded by homes. Later, in 1928, the Sam Davis Hotel was built on the corner lot between the Temple and Commerce Street.

The cornerstone ceremonies in 1874 included a parade, an address by former President Andrew Johnson and a dinner at the Maxwell House. The cost of the Temple was estimated at $50,000, much of which was raised by the Temple's Ladies Auxiliary.

Vine Street Temple, for which the cornerstone was placed in 1874
Historic Photos of Nashville

Vine Street Temple's roots go back to the 1840s when a group of Jews met for religious services at the home of Isaac Garretson on South Summer Street. The first Jewish congregation in Nashville was Khal Kodesh Mogen David (Star of David), started in 1854 in a room on North Market Street. An internal split in 1857 resulted in the formation of a second Jewish congregation, Khal Kodesh Ohava Emes.

In 1868 the two groups united and established the Congregation Ohabai Sholom (Lovers of Truth). By 1872, the congregation, with 61 members, felt strong enough to purchase the site on Vine Street for its permanent home. The amazing structure was noted for its concave ceiling, stained-glass windows, massive doors, and most impressive of all, a 145-foot-tall central dome.

In 1955 when the congregation moved to its present site on 5015 Harding Pike, the old site was sold and the building razed.

Civil War

Nathan Bedford Forrest Invites Capt. William Hicks "Red" Jackson to Command His Cavalry Regiment (August 1861)

The Contributor, 2022

On August 26, 1861, Howell E. Jackson, then practicing law on Front Street in Memphis, wrote his younger brother, Captain William Hicks "Billy" Jackson, then stationed at Randolph, Tennessee. Howell relayed to Billy that Nathan Bedford Forrest was in his office "a few days since" and informed Howell that he had been for some time raising a battalion of cavalry and that he had succeeded better than he expected and thought he "would soon have a full regiment of cavalry." Forrest did not think he was qualified to command a regiment and "would greatly prefer taking the second position under someone who was better qualified than himself" and spoke of Billy Jackson as the man he would like to have as colonel.

Howell wrote to Billy, "I told him I thought you would not hesitate to accept the command of the regiment if the same was tendered to you, and at his request I drop you this note to know what your views are upon this subject. You would not be required to surrender your present position until the new one was offered you and until the regiment was fully organized. Forrest is a bold, daring fellow as brave as a lion and would make an excellent Lt. Colonel."

I do not know what Billy Jackson's response was. He may not have received the letter for some time as he was no longer in Randolph when his brother's letter reached that river town. I do know that, on August 26, 1861, when Howell wrote him, Captain Jackson was in New Madrid, Missouri, with his battery that then amounted to about 130 men. On September 5th, Jackson's Battery moved across the river to Hickman, Kentucky, where they fired on Federal gunboats the next day. On the 7th, Jackson's Battery moved "over rough country roads" to Columbus, Kentucky. Later that day, at the Battle of Belmont, Captain Jackson was severely wounded "while assisting General [Gideon] Pillow to rally his brigade."

Either having not heard from Capt. Jackson or having learned that Jackson was in no position to accept his generous offer, Forrest succeeded, by the first week in October, in attracting to his standard eight companies of mounted volunteers which were organized into a battalion. He was elected lieutenant colonel. By the last week in October, the battalion was ready for

Gen. Nathan Bedford Forrest
Courtesy of Harper & Bros.,
Bedford Forrest

duty, and by November 4, Forrest's regiment of cavalry was at Fort Donelson. General Albert Sidney Johnston wrote, on November 4, "Give Forrest a chance and he will distinguish himself." That proved to be true in spades.

Of the three senior Confederate generals at Fort Donelson, two generals—John B. Floyd and Simon Bolivar Buckner—thought the situation there was hopeless. The third, General Gideon Pillow agreed with Forrest "that the army was there to fight, not surrender." However, they could not convince Floyd or Buckner to not surrender. After the last conference ended early Sunday morning, February 16, 1862,

Forrest stalked out of the room after announcing that he would not surrender himself nor his command. Forrest led his men out a road he had reconnoitered earlier, crossed a deep slough, saddle-skirt deep, and filed into the road to Cumberland Furnace. Not a single gun was fired at them, and no enemy had been heard or seen. Forrest took out approximately 1,000 men and realized that he had as much military sense as did Buckner, Floyd, and Pillow. Pillow and Floyd also escaped with some troops during the night, leaving Buckner to surrender to Gen. U. S. Grant on the 16th. On March 11, 1862, without a court of inquiry, Jefferson Davis removed Floyd from his command.

Many military critics pronounced Forrest to be the foremost cavalry officer ever produced in America.

William Hicks "Red" Jackson, recovered from his wound suffered at the Battle of Belmont, to become a brigadier general who commanded half of General Joseph Johnson's cavalry during the Atlanta campaign and commanded, in the Nashville campaign, all the Texas cavalry in General Forrest's department. Although he was never formally advanced to the grade of major general, Red Jackson led one of Forrest's two divisions at the close of the war.

Saint Cloud Hill and Fort Negley

The Contributor 5/22/2019

During the 1850s, Saint Cloud Hill was a well-known promontory one mile south of the city of Nashville. Its beautifully wooded slopes just east of the Franklin Turnpike served as a picnic area for the townsfolk.

The atmosphere of peace and quiet changed dramatically in 1862 following the late February surrender of Nashville to Union forces. Federal Captain James St. Clair Morton, U.S. Corps of Engineers, soon began to fortify Nashville. His plan was to build three large forts on the hills south of the city. Fort Morton, named for him, was to be built on the hill just north of the city reservoir. Fort Houston was to be built close to the intersection of today's Demonbreun and Division Streets. The third fort was to be built on Saint Cloud Hill. Forts Morton and Houston, expected to be large, permanent works, were never completed because Federal authorities were unable to find enough African Americans to build all three forts.

A block house, called Blockhouse Casino, was built on Kirkpatrick Hill, the site of today's Eighth Avenue Reservoir. The Union strategy was to demand that all large slave-owners furnish slaves to do the work. Elizabeth McGavock Harding, at Belle Meade, whose husband, William Giles, was a political prisoner at Fort Mackinac, Michigan, heard a rumor on about July 26, 1862, that Federal General William "Bull" Nelson "intends calling on the people of Davidson County to furnish 1,000 negroes to work on fortifications here, and the newspaper, called *The Union*, edited by a man named Mercer, from Kentucky, advocates it strongly." Elizabeth expected every day to be called on "for negroes to work on the fortifications." The call for them to do so came on Monday, August 11, 1862, when Mrs. Harding received an order "for 20 stout, able-bodied negro men, each one to be provided with axe, spade and shovel, and daily rations to be provided by Mrs. Harding." A day or so later, a number of Federals came out to Belle Meade and demanded twelve able-bodied men, duly furnished with implements, provisions, etc., to work on the fortifications. They told the slaves that, "if any negro voluntarily offers his services, when the work is done, he or they will be entitled to their freedom."

Twelve agreed to go and seven more slaves were rounded up down the road at Cousin Frank McGavock's plantation. David McGavock at Two Rivers lost "five or six to the ranks of the enemy." With only limited success at the county's large plantations, the Federals put cavalrymen outside three Black churches and grabbed young Black men as they came out. Nearly 2,000 Black men, both free and slave, were forced or agreed to go into service. They cleared Saint Cloud Hill of trees to open up lines of fire, blasted the solid rock and dug underground magazines. Expert slave stonemasons shaped the stone and laid thick masonry walls. Black women washed clothes, cooked food, and hauled away debris in wheelbarrows. Captain Morton said, "To the

Southwest view of Fort Negley in Nashville
Sketch by W. H. H. Fletcher, 12th Battery of Indiana Volunteers

credit of the colored population be it said, they worked manfully and cheerfully, with hardly an exception, and yet lay out upon the works at night under heavy guard, without blankets and eating only army rations."

Fort Negley was named for U.S. General James Scott Negley, who was, in 1862, commander of Federal forces in Nashville. The fort was constructed in only three months, being completed on December 7, 1862. It became the largest Union fort west of Washington, D.C., covering four acres. The polygonal-shaped structure measured approximately 600 by 300 feet. On May 15, 1865, Brig. Gen. Z. B. Tower submitted an inspection report to Maj. Gen. George H. Thomas. He wrote, "It is a very imposing fort and its appearance alone would keep an enemy at a good distance." The Confederates never attacked; however, it is likely that the opening salvos of the Battle of Nashville were fired from the fort. The Union army abandoned Fort Negley after 1867, but the fort did not remain vacant.

The Klu Klux Klan held secret meetings in its blockhouse until 1869 when former Confederate General Nathan B. Forrest, head of the Klan, led Nashville Den Klan members to the fort where they burned their robes and officially disbanded.

The next major activity came in 1887 and 1888 when some of the stones at Fort Negley were taken to build the Eighth Avenue South Reservoir, which was completed on the former site of Blockhouse Casino on August 24, 1889. Again, Fort Negley was ignored until 1936 and 1937 when the Works Progress Administration (WPA) restored the fort. Abandoned again, it fell into ruins. Finally, in 1998, Michael Emrick, a historical architect, called Fort Negley an "absolute phenomenal resource" to generate tourism in the city. In 2002, the city responded by allocating one million dollars to totally rebuild the fort. This was eventually done and, several years ago, most of the trees on the slopes of the fort were removed. Although this received some criticism, I agreed with the decision as the fort looks today more like it did in 1862 when the trees were removed to clear lines of fire.

U. S. Army Hospital No. 8

The Contributor 6/6/2016

This was Nashville's largest military hospital during the Civil War. On January 4, 1863, one day after the Confederate retreat from Murfreesboro following the Battle of Stones River, the U.S. Army commandeered Nashville's First Presbyterian Church for use as a U.S. Army Hospital. The Army returned the building to the church officers on August 19, 1863, but confiscated it again on October 14, 1863, and used it, the Masonic Hall across Spring Street, and the Cumberland Presbyterian Church on Summer Street at Cumberland Alley as the city's largest military hospital until April 27, 1865. The pews in the church's sanctuary were removed so that cots could be placed there for convalescing Union soldiers, mostly Midwesterners. Other soldiers were housed on cots downstairs. On the east side of the church, a two-story wooden latrine served the ill and wounded soldiers.

On April 12, 1864, Elvira J. Powers, a volunteer nurse from Massachusetts, visited U.S. Hospital No. 8. She toured the part of the hospital in the Masonic Hall first. After passing the security guard, she ascended a broad flight of stairs to a second-floor ward where she met a matron from Ann Arbor, Michigan, who was responsible for building maintenance. The matron's staff consisted of seven Negro women and two Negro men. Powers saw only a few patients. One was a fifteen-year-old boy, who asked the matron to bring him some dried peaches. She agreed to do so but would not accept his offer to pay for the peaches with money hidden under his pillow.

Powers next crossed the street to visit patients in First Presbyterian Church, which she had been told, "was notable for the promulgation of secession sentiments from its pulpit in other days." She and a fellow nurse responded by singing "The Star-Spangled Banner" accompanied by the church organ. This, Elvira said, gave "much pleasure to the sick and wounded soldiers."

In September, when Powers was back in Nashville, the matron in the U.S. Hospital No. 8 was Miss Annie Bell, described as "possessing a really noble and independent nature."

On July 1, 1865, Captain T. Wing, of the Quartermaster's Department in Nashville, gave Robert Lusk, treasurer of First Presbyterian

Civil War soldiers used the Masonic Hall as part of Hospital No. 8.
National Archives, *Cities Under the Gun*

Church, a check for $7,500 to settle the church's claim for damages done to the church during its use as a U.S. Army hospital. The minutes of Deacons meetings indicate the money was accepted and used for repairs, including the purchasing of new cushions, repair of the church organ by its builder from Boston, interior painting and replacement, and varnishing of the pews that had been stored elsewhere. It took the congregation until

Sunday, November 12, 1865, to restore the church building to a condition suitable for worship. That morning, for the first time in three years, the doors were thrown open for the worship of God.

In 1914, Congress voted to give the church an additional $1,200 for war-time damages.

I grew up in First Presbyterian Church, and remember seeing elderly couples from the Midwest who, in the summers during the 1940s, visited the church to see where their grandfathers, Union soldiers, recuperated from battle wounds and illnesses.

An Alternative View of the Fort Pillow Massacre

The Contributor 5/8/2019

In early 1864, Confederate sympathizers living in Brownsville and nearby West Tennessee towns complained to General Nathan Bedford Forrest about deprivations made by Major Booth's 13th Tennessee Cavalry operating out of Fort Pillow in Lauderdale County, Tennessee, forty miles north of Memphis. His were Union soldiers, both Black and White, with many of the Whites hailing from the West Tennessee counties immediately west of the Tennessee River, where the land was poor and the small farmers had no slaves. Some were ex-Confederates, who had changed sides.

Forrest agreed to help. He assembled his troops in Brownsville on April 11 and undertook a forced march that covered the 38 miles to Fort Pillow, putting his men there by daylight the next morning. Early on April 12, the advance guard surprised the pickets at Fort Pillow and captured all but two or three who gave the alarm to Col. Booth, the fort commander.

The fort, which 557 Union troops occupied, had been built by the Confederates in 1861, primarily to command the Mississippi River, whose channel came near the fort, and to be the last in a chain of defenses protecting Memphis. The inner works had parapets eight feet high and a ditch six feet deep and twelve feet wide. It was defective, however, because it was easily approachable from the south by a ravine that ran close to the fort. Also, less than sixty yards from the redoubt there were huts occupied "as quarters by the garrison." Confederates could take shelter behind them. From the southeast and east, there were steep-sided ravines that gave assailants shelter from view.

Booth's men's armament consisted of two ten-pounder Parrott rifled guns, two twelve-pound howitzers, and two six-pound rifled bore field pieces. His garrison consisted of 295 White and 262 Black troops, not nearly enough to properly man the outer works so they were concentrated within the redoubt.

Early on April 12, Col. McCullough's Confederates seized a position about half mile south of the fort close to the river. Wilson's regiment deployed directly in front of the fort while Bell's Brigade deployed to the north along Coal Creek close to its mouth.

When General Forrest arrived about 9 a.m. he immediately went forward to reconnoiter. While doing so, he had two horses killed under him and a third wounded, badly bruising him. Forrest quickly realized that the ravine leading up to the southern face of the fort would provide cover as the Federal artillery could not depress sufficiently to command it. He ordered the ravine occupied.

Forrest also realized that two ridges four to five hundred feet to the east and northeast of the fort gave excellent cover to his sharpshooters who could from there completely command the fort's interior.

Confederate Brigadier General James Chalmers, who had arrived earlier, had already chased Union pickets from the outer works back to their main work, giving up their rifle pits in its front. The rifle pits were immediately occupied by Confederates. Now, the line of involvement was complete from a swollen Coal Creek north of the fort to the river bank south of the fort. Forrest had about 1,500 men. He and Chalmers realized that, with their overwhelming force, they could easily carry the inner works.

To avoid having to storm the fort, Forrest called for a cessation of fire and deputized Capt. Walter Goodman to bear a flag of truce to Major Booth, whom Forrest assumed was still in command. Actually, Booth had been killed about the time Forrest arrived. A much less experienced officer, Major William F. Bradford, was actually in command.

The terms of surrender were that the entire garrison, Black and White, would be treated as prisoners of war. Usually, Black Federal soldiers had not been so treated, instead being considered slaves and returned to their former owners. Goodman and his small party discussed this point among themselves and asked Forrest for a clarification. Forrest and Chalmers both said the Black troops would be considered prisoners of war. The parlay took place just outside the fort. Forrest instructed Goodman to tell the fort commander that he must receive an answer in twenty minutes. The inexperienced Union commander, Major Bradford—pretending to be the deceased Booth—asked if the Federal gunboats were included in the surrender. The answer was no. Forrest added that, if the Federals didn't surrender, he could not be held responsible for any atrocities because of the extreme animosity existing between the Tennesseans of the two commands.

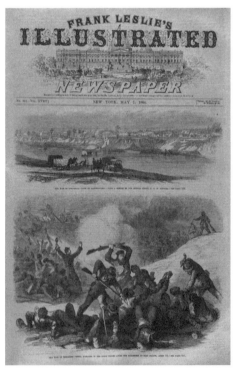

Bradford consulted with the commanders of two gunboats, the *New Era* and *Olive Branch,* who agreed to provide cover and take on fort defenders if they were overrun. To prevent the two Federal gunboats from doing that, Forrest dispatched a squadron of McCullough's Brigade to

Etchings of Fort Pillow in *Frank Leslie's Illustrated Newspaper,* New York, May 7, 1864

occupy old Confederate trenches under the river bluff just below the southern face of the fort. They effectively kept the gunboats away. Nevertheless, the presence of the gunboats gave Bradford the courage to decline to surrender. He was sufficiently worried about his troops' ability to resist that he asked Goodman to prove that Forrest was actually there. Bradford also authorized giving whiskey to his defenders, who were rightfully afraid of Robert E. Lee's most aggressive and best general.

To prove that he was there, Forrest moved to an exposed position, where he could be easily seen from the fort. Bradford made two regrettable decisions. One was to give whiskey to his frightened enlisted men, and the other was to not accept a surrender that would enable his men, Black and White, to be considered prisoners of war and paroled aboard a steamer in the vicinity. Bradford gave Goodman a note declining to surrender. Surprised, Forrest immediately ordered an assault by his Mississippians, Tennesseans, and Texans, who were already close to the fort. The assault took only a few minutes. It was less difficult than it would have been because a number of the Union soldiers were intoxicated. Whiskey may bolster your courage, but it certainly does not steady your aim.

With the Union flag still flying over the fort, the surviving Union soldiers tried to flee from the back of the fort down the riverbank, having been told that they would be protected by the covering fire of the two gunboats, and could escape on those boats. In this wild scramble, some Union soldiers threw away their rifles, some tried to surrender, while some fired over their shoulders at the pursuing Confederates. Suddenly, the Union soldiers, Black and White, realized the gunboats were not there, having been intimidated by McCullough's men. Many jumped in the river and tried to swim away only to either drown or be picked off by Confederate rifleman. Others veered south where McCullough's men awaited them. Still others tried to flee north to the mouth of swollen Coal Creek, where they were gunned down by Confederate Col. Clark Barteau's men.

As soon as it was apparent that the assault was successful, Forrest rode into the fort with Col. John Overton, had the Union flag taken down and ordered that firing cease. Within fifteen minutes firing ceased and soon details of captured Union soldiers were ordered to bury their own dead.

Among those captured was Major Bradford. He was paroled to bury his brother and then placed in custody of Colonel McCullough, who shared his supper with him and gave him a bed in his own quarters. Bradford pledged not to attempt an escape that night. He did escape, however, but was soon caught wearing civilian clothes. Under the guard of five Confederate soldiers, he was led to captivity. On the road, they killed him and told their superior officer that Bradford was killed while trying to escape. Unfortunately, Forrest believed their lie.

The result of the capture of the hapless fort was that of Bradford's 550 or so men, some 150 had surrendered, about 100 were wounded in and around the fort, and were later handed over to a Federal gunboat under a flag of truce. The remaining 300 or so were either killed or drowned. Forrest reported that "the river was dyed with the blood of the slaughtered for 200 yards."

Confederate losses were minimal. Fourteen Confederate enlisted men and officers were killed, and sixty-eight were wounded. With a truce in force, the Federal steamer *Platte Valley* came up and took aboard at least seventy officers and men who had been paroled. Few escaped.

After the fight, General Chalmers put his main force in motion toward Brownsville and a little later he withdrew with his staff and escort, leaving at Fort Pillow only the Federal dead.

The terrible fate of Fort Pillow led to a "furious storm of invective against Forrest throughout the North." He was accused of refusing to take prisoners, of having shot down "helpless and disarmed men," and having butchered "whole batches" of captives, primarily Black men. A subcommittee of Congress was quickly assembled to investigate. They issued a report on "the Fort Pillow Massacre" undoubtedly to damage the Confederate cause in the eyes of the civilized world. The report said (1) that Forrest took advantage of the truce to advance his men forward, (2) that, after the capture of the fort, an indiscriminate slaughter took place, (3) that wounded men were burned to death in their barracks or tents, and (4) that others were buried alive. Forrest and his biographers refuted the claims, pointing out that the Federal commanders never surrendered. The Confederate position was that it was a legitimate act of war to fire on those attempting to escape whether they were armed or not. One problem the Black men had was that most of their officers were killed in the assault and they had no one to guide them. There were wild stories of a wounded 13th Battalion quartermaster being nailed to a wall after he was wounded and burned alive. Forrest, who had long since left, and his subordinates did not, I think, order the murder of captives. They did not do enough, however, to stop individual soldiers from taking out their vengeance by murdering helpless prisoners, including Major Bradford.

In Brownsville, the citizens of all classes welcomed the Confederates at the courthouse as heroes, having delivered them from the insults, harassments, and annoyances of the Union garrison at Fort Pillow. The controversy continues to this day. I personally feel that Major Bradford was almost as much to blame as Forrest by (1) refusing to surrender to an overwhelming force led by a legendary Confederate general, who promised to take Black soldiers as prisoners of war, and (2) by giving whiskey to his frightened enlisted men to boost their courage before the assault.

Clubs

Women Launched
Nashville's Centennial Club (1905)

The Contributor 1/3/2017

Women launched Nashville's Centennial Club in 1905. The ladies' club, an outgrowth of the successful 1897 Tennessee Centennial Exposition, was organized in 1905 by the women who had represented Middle Tennessee on the Women's Board of the Centennial Exposition. Mrs. John Hill Eakin, one of Nashville's most able civic leaders, was its first president. Sadie Le Sueur (Mrs. Thomas Randle) was executive secretary of the club from 1936 into the 1950s. The Centennial Club met in a spacious brick clubhouse on Eighth Avenue South in downtown Nashville. Le Sueur planned elaborately executed luncheons, teas and receptions for the club, and was praised for her deviled oysters and cheese dreams.

When the Centennial Club moved in the early 1970s from its downtown location to its present location at 2805 Abbott-Martin Road, my mother-in-law, Henriette Jackson, was responsible for the landscaping.

The Centennial Club, which may be the oldest ladies' civic club in the state, has had excellent speakers over the years. In recent years, my wife, Irene, a club member, has been in a painting class at the club taught by Paul Zeppelin.

Ladies normally wear dresses, and men wear coats and ties to events held at the Centennial Club. Until recent years, a female member was not admitted if she showed up in a pants suit. The present manager is Tom Bogan and the current president is Jane (Mrs. Thomas F.) Corcoran.

Now on Abbott-Martin Road in Nashville, the Centennial Club was organized in 1905 and met on Eighth Avenue South.
The Centennial Club of Nashville

Coal Miners' Strike

Miners Strike and Lose Their Leader

The Contributor 9/11/2019

In the early 1930s, the cause of organized labor in Southern Appalachia received little public support. Most legislators in Tennessee considered unions to be socialist or even communist organizations.

The Wilder strike began in the summer of 1932 when three coal companies owned all the coal mines around the Twinton and Crawford communities in Overton County and the Wilder and Davidson communities in Fentress County. The New York–based Brier Hill Collieries owned the mines at Twinton and Crawford in Overton County; Hubert Patterson operated the mines at Davidson; and W. D. Boyer and L. L. Shivers managed the area's largest mines at Wilder for the Nashville-based Fentress Coal & Coke Company. The Depression forced Brier Hill Collieries to close its Twinton and Crawford mines early in the summer of 1932. The managers of the mines at Wilder announced they would not renew their contracts unless the members of the UMW local union's members agreed to a 20 percent cut in wages. Union miners, who had resented unhealthy conditions in the mines and mining camps for years, rejected the demand and went on strike. A union spokesperson said: "We would rather starve out in the open than starve to death in the mines." The mines remained closed until mid-October in 1932 when nonunion miners and a handful of union members resumed work at the Wilder mines under the protection of armed guards.

For the next seven months, until June 1933, the violence at the Wilder strike was comparable to the violence between coal miners and operators in "Bloody" Harlan County, Kentucky. In November 1932, Gov. Henry Horton dispatched nearly 200 National Guardsmen into the area, but the presence of the inexperienced guardsmen, who were quite young, did little to calm the situation.

Myles Horton, the founder of the Highlander Folk School, established months earlier in Summerfield, Tennessee (a small community near Monteagle), took an interest in the miners' plight, and went to Wilder on Thanksgiving Day, 1932. There, he shared a meager

Sympathetic to the Union, Myles Horton (right), his Highlander Folk School staff, and others helped support coal miners by providing food and clothing in 1933 in Wilder (Fentress County, Tennessee). Courtesy of the Heritage Center, Tracy City, Tennessee

Thanksgiving dinner with Barney Graham, president of the Wilder UMW Local. The next day Myles was deeply moved by the suffering he witnessed in the depressed mountain community. That afternoon, while waiting for a bus to take him home to Summerfield, State Police Captain Hubert Crawford arrested Myles Horton and took him to the local police headquarters, where his notes on the strike were seized and he was charged with "coming here and getting information and going back and teaching it [at Highlander Folk School]."

In early December of 1932, Fentress Coal Company officials secured a sweeping injunction against the local union, effectively deciding the fate of the strike. The guardsmen left Wilder shortly before Christmas but returned in January after violence again erupted. After an uneasy truce in 1933, the staff at Highlander Folk School and others sympathetic to the Union cause began providing relief to the striking miners and their families. A few miners were reluctant to accept the desperately needed food and clothing from Horton, his associate Don West, and the students because they had been told Myles Horton was "red." However, the assistance offered convinced many of the miners of Myles Horton's good intentions. The Highlander staff believed they could not only "save" Wilder, but also give inspiration to "Southern labor at large." This did not happen. Early in 1933, more and more striking miners returned to work. It became obvious to Myles Horton and West that the strike would only last as long as Graham was able to hold the union together.

After the Tennessee National Guard left for the second time on February 17, 1933, there was another wave of ambushes, dynamite explosions, fires, guns, battles, holdups, and whippings. To prove that, if it were not for Graham and "outside influences," a majority of the strikers would return to work, Fentress Coal Company managers published a letter written by a Highlander student who said that "the historic mission of the working class is to destroy the capitalist system."

In mid-April, Myles Horton learned of a plan by company guards to kill Graham. He warned state officials in Nashville, including Gov. Henry Horton, who failed to heed his warnings. Two weeks later, on April 30, 1933, Graham was murdered. Myles later said that, after

Graham's murder, which was never solved, "If I hadn't been a radical, that would have made me a radical right there." A day after Graham's death, nearly 300 miners returned to work without a union contract, and under heavy guard.

In June 1933, the *Chattanooga Times* editor noted that "Blood Wilder" was fast becoming "ragged Wilder, hungry Wilder, desperate Wilder," whose people could no longer exist without some form of relief. Banking, telephone, transportation, medical and educational facilities all but disappeared at Wilder. Fentress Coal Company was free to continue with what Myles Horton called "their ruthless exploitation of its workers." Some miners escaped to find jobs at TVA's the Clinch River Dam at Cove Creek.

President Roosevelt's Civilian Conservation Corps helped on the Plateau, in Chattanooga, and elsewhere across the country. At one time during the Depression, the unemployment rate in Grundy County, a coal mining county south of Overton County, where the Highlander Folk School was located, reached 72 percent. The unemployment rates in Overton and Fentress Counties must have been almost as high. Had not President Roosevelt ushered in his progressive New Deal, I believe we might have had a revolution. To give you an idea of how desperate Cumberland Plateau blue collar workers were, here is a letter, written in 1934 from a Grundy County bug-wood striker to the President of the United States:

> "Dear Sir: If your children were shriveling up before your eyes because there wasn't enough for them to eat and you had tried every way you could get a paying job or enough relief for them to live on, maybe you would be writing this letter instead of us. Folks like you who own things that make money have a hard time understanding what the working class is up against. We are not blaming you: That's how the system works. But you can't blame us for wanting to live even when it doesn't pay the rich to hire us. We are American citizens and we've got rights."

Communities/Cities

Shackle Island Is Pure Middle Tennessee

The Contributor 1/22/2020

Many Nashvillians have heard of Shackle Island but most have no idea of where it is and what made it important. An article in *The Tennessean* on March 29, 1964, had the headline "Shackle Island Is Pure Middle Tennessee."

To reach Shackle Island, head north on I-65 from Nashville. Get off at the Long Hollow Pike exit and drive northeast on that road through the hills and past stone fences and a branch of Drake's Creek. In time, you will reach the old Beech Church, Drakes Creek, and Shackle Island—all timeless landmarks of rural Sumner County. This fertile, well-watered, and long-settled country is five miles south of a great ridge, which divides Sumner County into two parts: the northern part is on the Highland Rim while Shackle Island is in the Middle Tennessee basin halfway between Goodlettsville to the west and Gallatin to the east.

A natural question is how Shackle Island got its name. The most generally accepted theory is that a man named Shackle, with his family, operated a grist mill on Drakes Creek for William Montgomery, who lived near the creek. A small island near the Montgomery home came to be known as Shackle Island. William Montgomery, a surveyor, completed his big, brick house in 1804, using bricks made on the place. Rafters were numbered and pegged together. Woodwork around the fireplace at "Old Brick" is credited to Robert Taylor, a local craftsman who crafted it of yellow poplar. The ornamental wood-work was later painted white. Old Brick remained in the Montgomery family for 138 years until it was sold to Jim Ralph.

William Montgomery's house "Old Brick" on Tyree Springs Road
A Pictorial History of Sumner County, Tennessee

The other historic site you must see at Shackle Island is "Old Beech" Cumberland Presbyterian Church and its ancient cemetery. Initially, the site of a campground and a log church, Old Beech was organized as a Presbyterian Church in 1795 by the Rev. Thomas Craighead. It became a Cumberland Presbyterian Church in about 1810. The present stone building with walls three feet thick was built in 1828. Fire has twice destroyed the interior of the church, but each time, it was rebuilt. One of the oldest graves in the cemetery is that of a Revolutionary War soldier, John McMurtry, who was born in 1752 and died in 1841.

Dr. Robert N. Buchanan Jr., a physician, who lived on Belle Meade Boulevard before his death some years ago, grew up on a farm near Shackle Island. He once told me that he went to Goodlettsville High School before attending Vanderbilt, where he was competing with boys, many of whom went to private prep schools, who were academically ahead of him. He caught up, however, and had a long and distinguished career as a Nashville physician.

Dr. Buchanan's father, Dr. Robert N. Buchanan Sr., had a farm near Shackle Island and practiced medicine there for forty years. He was a graduate of the University of Nashville Medical School in 1905. His brother Thomas Buchanan graduated from Bethel College in McKendree, Tennessee, and went on to become a Cumberland Presbyterian minister. Thomas was pastor of "Old Beech" Church early in the twentieth century. He was killed when he was struck by a lightning bolt in about 1913. Thomas and Robert Buchanan were the sons of John Price Buchanan, who was governor of Tennessee from 1891 until 1893. His ancestor, Major John Buchanan, had a stockade beside Mill Creek where one of the most remarkable Indian battles of the old Southwest was fought. Today, Robert N. Buchanan III is a Nashville attorney and president of the Tennessee Historical Society.

How Littlelot Got Its Name

The Contributor 3/2/2022

This village, located eleven miles west of Centerville in Hickman County, Tennessee, lies at an elevation of 550 feet in the fertile Duck River Valley. It received its name in 1815 when a prosperous slave and landowner, Hugh McCabe, who owned hundreds of acres, gave a quarter of an acre for a church and school. The village authorities thought that the piece of donated land was much too small to have "a big name" so they named their village Littlelot.

Littlelot had, in 1876, a population of between forty and fifty. In the village there were a general store, cotton-gin, saw and grist mills,

Photo by K. C. Potter

and a blacksmith shop. The Methodists and Christians had churches and there was a Masonic Lodge, and a school, Green Wood Academy.

In 1918, Littlelot was described as being in "the hog and hominy" part of the state near the Duck River. The article went on to say the area had "beautiful scenery and everything to make one feel so free that he will not want to leave. No better people on earth."

There was a Littelot Normal School of Music in the village in 1918. Board could be had in the best homes in the village for $3.50 to $4.00 per week. Tuition for the twenty-week course was $3.00 for children over fifteen years of age and $2.00 for those under fifteen. The school's president was C. B. Wilson.

Why Did the City of Belle Meade Incorporate?

The Contributor 12/22/2021

Many readers of *The Contributor* probably don't know why the City of Belle Meade incorporated in 1938. Here is why. Peggy Henry Joyce, whose father, Douglas Henry, was Belle Meade's first mayor, told me there were two reasons. One was that most residents in the Belle Meade Park subdivisions, largely developed by Johnson Bransford and Luke Lea, did not want commercial establishments on Belle Meade Boulevard. In the thirties, Mr. Cornett had a Pan Am service station on Harding Road near where the Belle Meade City Hall is today. He made known his interest in building a new service station on Belle Meade Boulevard.

The other reason was that Henry C. Beck, an Atlanta real estate developer, intended to build Nashville's first garden-style apartments in the heart of Belle Meade Park. Beck, whose company is now headquartered in Dallas, visited Nashville probably in the winter of 1937–38 to inspect the site. It was a triangular section of land on the north side of Harding Place and in the triangle between Jackson and Belle Meade boulevards just across the street from the Belle Meade Country Club. Beck had the financing, $700,000, from a New York City insurance company to finance the project.

Belle Meade Park residents were livid about the possibility of having a filling station and a large apartment complex in Belle Meade Park. They called for a meeting to consider how to stop the projects. The first meeting was held on February 10, 1938, at the Belle Meade Country Club. A second meeting was held on February 25. At that meeting, chaired by Robert C. Webster, he appointed Harry H. Corson, Paul F. Eve M.D., Morton B. Howell, John F. Hunt, and Alfred D. Sharp to investigate the feasibility of incorporating as a city as the most effective means of halting the projects.

Realizing how opposed most residents of Belle Meade Park seemed to be about his proposal, Henry Beck backed off and, on February 10, Beck's representative, Paul A. Rye, announced that the real estate company, "thought it unwise to proceed with the project in this section." Instead, Henry C. Beck & Co. purchased a larger piece of land, owned by Rogers Caldwell, at 920 Woodmont Boulevard just west of a branch of Brown's Creek and built there a two-story apartment complex named Woodmont Terrace. It still remains today as Nashville's oldest garden-style apartment complex.

Belle Meade City Hall, late 1980s   Courtesy of City of Belle Meade

On October 28, 1938, 270 residents of Belle Meade Park voted in favor of incorporation while 170 qualified voters voted against incorporation. One of the earliest actions taken by Belle Meade's first three commissioners—Douglas Henry, Robert C. Cooney, and Alex B. Stevenson—was to pass an ordinance that no more than two families could live in a single residence and that no commercial businesses could be established in the City of Belle Meade.

Nashville MSA Shows Record Growth in 2020 Census

The Contributor 9/29/2021

In recent decades it has been appropriate to measure the size of America's larger cities by the size of their metropolitan statistical areas (MSAs). This is because our largest cities tend to spill over into increasingly large metropolitan areas. A striking example is the Atlanta MSA, which in 2020 sprawled over twenty-eight counties. In Tennessee, the Nashville MSA, the state's most heavily populated, included these twelve counties: Davidson, Cannon, Cheatham, Dickson, Macon, Maury, Robertson, Rutherford, Smith, Sumner, Williamson, and Wilson.

The Memphis MSA was the state's second largest. In 2020, it included Fayette, Shelby, and Tipton Counties in Tennessee; DeSoto, Marshall, Tate, and Tunica in Mississippi; and Crittenton in Arkansas.

Chattanooga had six counties in its MSA. They included Hamilton, Marion, and Sequatchie in Tennessee; and Dade, Catoosa, and Walker County in Georgia.

The Knoxville MSA in 2020 included Anderson, Knox, Blount, and Union counties; while the Clarksville MSA included Montgomery and Stewart Counties in Tennessee and Christian and Trigg Counties in Kentucky.

The Nashville MSA was the 36th largest in the country in 2020. It grew by 20.86 percent since 2010. Only two MSAs in the country that were larger than Nashville grew faster between 2010 and 2020: the Austin, Texas, MSA, which was the 28th largest in the country, grew by 33.04 percent and the Orlando, Florida, MSA, which was the 22nd largest in the country grew by 25.25 percent.

Down in the Nations

The Contributor early 2022

This interesting section of West Nashville, originally referred to as "Down in the Nation" (singular), came about as a result of a new Tennessee State Prison being completed in 1898 at the end of Esplanade Boulevard, soon renamed Centennial Boulevard. This was a state highway built from the end of Jefferson Street to the new penitentiary.

The Tennessee State Penitentiary, ca. 1902
Collection of Ridley Wills II

In 1898, an industrious carpenter named Walter Wright began building shotgun type houses in this area. They were three rooms deep, and primarily rented to the families of state prisoners who wanted to live near the penal institution and who could only afford cheap rent. State penitentiary guards and their families also lived there. Being a poor class of people, the area became a high crime area over the years, and the young boys who lived there were considered "daring roughnecks." The area was called "Down in the Nation" or "The Nation." Outsiders seldom went there. As most of these families were needy, the school teachers at the closest elementary school made flour sack underwear for the children who attended classes there.

I suspect that the area was named "The Nation" for the Cherokee, Chickasaw, and other Indian nations whose warriors attended a treaty with the Cumberland settlers in May and June 1783. It was held at a large spring on James Robertson's land along Richland Creek about four miles from Nashville and a few hundred yards from the Charlotte Pike.

Today, this area of town is now called "The Nations" (plural), and a majority of the original houses have been razed and replaced with the thin, two- and three-story townhouses, many of which have garages in front of the house with a narrow staircase to the living quarters on the upper floor or floors. My granddaughter, Meade Wills, who graduated from Harpeth Hall in 2012, tells me that a number of her classmates live in "The Nations." The area has definitely been greatly upgraded and is a budding dining and entertainment hub. Crime too has substantially reduced.

Epidemics

Influenza Epidemic of 1918

The Contributor 4/1/2020

The influenza epidemic that began in 1918 was considered the deadliest in modern history, infecting an estimated 500 million people worldwide—about one-third of the population of the planet—and killed an estimated 20 to 50 million victims, including some 675,000 Americans. It was caused by an H1N1 influenza virus with genes of avian origin. A myth was that the epidemic originated in Spain, and those who believed this called it the "Spanish Flu Epidemic," though there was no evidence to suggest that it came from Spain at all.

The epidemic, which came in three waves, first hit Europe. The flu infected 25 percent of American troops during World War I, killing more than 1 million men. More than one half of the casualties from The Great War were caused by the epidemic. There were no drugs or vaccines to treat it. When the influenza hit, doctors were hard pressed to help their patients.

The Influenza Epidemic of 1918 impacted my family directly. Early in 1918, my grandfather, Dr. Matt Buckner, was practicing medicine with his good friend, Dr. Thomas Shadrach Weaver, in the Jackson Building on the corner of Church Street and Fifth Avenue

Capt. Matt Buckner and his wife, Elizabeth, on the front steps of their home at 2000 Terrace Place, 1918
Collection of Ridley Wills II

North. Early that summer, Buckner, age forty-seven, who had three daughters still at home, volunteered to go in the U.S. Army. He received a commission in the U. S. Army Medical Corps as a Captain and was assigned to Camp McClellan, outside Anniston, Alabama. There he was named head of the Department of Sanitation, a temporary assignment as, at that point, there was not enough work in the wards to put him there.

The situation changed dramatically the first week in October 1918, when the Fort McClellan Hospital was getting loads of influenza and pneumonia patients. By October 13, there were 3,836 patients in hospital rooms and along covered boardwalks. Matt's ward was Pneumonia Ward #17. That day, he wrote to his wife, Elizabeth, telling her "I have never seen so many desperately sick men in my whole life as I have seen in the past two weeks." The same day, Dr. Buckner learned of Tom Weaver's death at Fort Oglethorpe of influenza. He also worried about his oldest daughter, Mary Harding, who, as a volunteer, was riding out to Old Hickory every day from Union Station to work in the Black Powder Plant.

In his letter to his wife, Dr. Buckner wrote that we treat "all our influenza patients with iron, quinine, and strychnine." By October 16, the hospital's patent load topped 4,000 as the influenza swept across the country. On October 21, Matt wrote home that he had forty pneumonia cases in his ward as the influx of new cases had decreased over the past three days. By the end of October, the situation continued to lighten up. Then the hospital was discharging about 1,000 patients a month and taking in between twenty or thirty a day. They were losing about six patients a day. Mostly the fatalities came when men, already weakened by influenza, caught pneumonia. On the 27th, Matt had twenty-seven men in his ward. He was weary and hoped to be home by Christmas.

On December 6, Buckner was given responsibility for all the wards on the west side of the hospital as well as the isolation ward. He did get Christmas leave and spent it at home with Elizabeth and their daughters. There, he enjoyed scotch stew and waffles for breakfast.

Buckner returned to Fort McClellan in late December, where he remained until March 10, 1919, when he received orders to report at the Embarkation Hospital at Camp Stewart, Virginia, three miles from Newport News. This hospital was still busy taking care of sick soldiers coming home from Europe.

Dr. Buckner was finally released from service on June 27, 1919, when he left Norfolk at 10:50 a.m. on a Southern Railroad train. He

Capt. Matt G. Buckner, MD, and his medical staff at Fort McClelland, Alabama, 1918   Collection of Ridley Wills II

arrived in Nashville on Saturday morning. Matt was officially discharged at Camp Zachary Taylor in Louisville on July 13, 1919, exactly one year after he entered the service.

Tom Weaver's son, Thomas S. Weaver Jr., also became a physician. He was a pediatrician for our three sons. Our youngest son, Thomas Weaver Wills, who cofounded *The Contributor*, was named for Dr. Weaver.

Expositions

Tennessee Centennial Exposition

The Contributor 6/5/2019

The first person to publicly advocate holding a Centennial Exposition in Tennessee was a Nashville attorney, Douglas Anderson. He did so in a letter to the *Chattanooga Times* on August 10, 1892. A presidential election in 1892 and a recession were two reasons that nothing happened as a result of his suggestion. A year later, Captain W. C. Smith, also of Nashville, wrote the board of directors of Nashville's Commercial Club promoting the idea of celebrating the first centennial of Tennessee's admission into the Union by holding a great exposition in Nashville in 1896. This time there was a favorable response, following the lead of the Nashville daily press. Smith was named chairman of a committee of twenty-five to pursue the matter. The committee recommended that a grand exposition showcasing the resources, products, manufactures, arts, industry and history of the state be held in Nashville from May 1, 1896 until November 1, 1896, and that a board of directors, sixty in number, be named to manage the effort. This materialized and, on July 24, 1894, an executive committee was elected. Major A. W. Wills was named the Director General in this formative period. The committee asked the State's Legislature to appropriate $350,000 and went to Washington, D.C. to lobby for federal aid.

On the Fourth of July 1895, only $62,635 had been subscribed. Of this, $50,000 came from Davidson County. The executive committee met on May 18, 1895 to, "determine whether we should continue the effort to hold the exposition, or abandon it." Although the situation was desperate, the committee members unanimously voted to go on, although they had no idea where the money would come from. The committee resigned in July, feeling that reorganization at that time would be beneficial. A new committee of nine was appointed to consider the advisability of reorganizing the Centennial Exposition Company. The members voted to do so and, before the meeting adjourned, $12,649 had been raised. By July 20, a total of $165,000 had been subscribed.

On July 23, 1895, the directors met at Watkins Hall, where they elected Major John Thomas president. Before the meeting adjourned, Major Thomas appointed an executive committee. A week later, Major Eugene C. Lewis was elected Director General. In September, Lewis outlined his plans. He proposed that the main exposition building be an exact reproduction of the Parthenon in Athens, Greece, and that other buildings be grouped around it. In October 1895, the executive committee instructed the Director General to advertise at once for plans and specifications from architects for the Parthenon, Transportation Building, and auditorium. These plans were approved on November 29, 1895. This would not have happened had not the Nashville City Council voted unanimously to submit to the voters of the city a proposal that the city subscribe $100,000 to the Centennial. The proposal was approved. Soon, employees of the NC&StL Railroad and the Gerst Brewing Company subscribed $7,500 and $2,635 respectively. Employees of other Nashville companies followed suit. Despite the gratifying support, the management of the Exposition company realized that having an opening in 1896 was impossible. Accordingly, they voted to postpone the opening to May 1, 1897.

Director General Lewis reported to the executive committee on June 8, 1896, that disbursements amounted to $204,354.83 and that the sum of $106,926.86 had to be raised to pay for the work then in hand and under contract. Nashville's two major railroads, the L&N and

Fine Arts Building, better known as the Parthenon
The Official History of the Tennessee Centennial Exposition

the NC&StL, came through with gifts of $25,000 each. The NC&StL also built a terminal at the north entrance to the exposition at a cost of $15,000 and installed a magnificent exhibit at a cost of $10,000. Work began on a Negro Building and a Machinery Hall. During the long construction period, the pressure on Director General Lewis intensified. To lessen his burden, the executive committee on April 15, 1897, named Dr. William L. Dudley, of Vanderbilt, director of affairs. He proved to be a strong right arm for Lewis.

Three issues were paramount in the minds of the Centennial executive committee—the idea of incorporating Centennial City in order to give it police power and remove its control from political influence; a financial appropriation from the national government; and an appropriation from the state legislature. All three were achieved although the appropriations were not as large as had been hoped.

On December 19, 1896, the federal government appropriated $130,000 for the construction of a building and for a national exhibit. The bill was passed contingent on the Centennial raising $500,000 in bona fide subscriptions from individuals, cities, counties, and states.

By the end of the month, the $27,000 needed was raised thanks largely to the people of Nashville. Next came the struggle with the state legislature for an appropriation. While $350,000 had been discussed, a more cautious ask of $100,000 was decided upon. After a bitter struggle, the legislature appropriated $50,000 of which $30,000 was designated for the construction of the Agriculture Building. The third hurdle was the incorporation of Centennial City, which would allow the exposition to sell intoxicating liquors. Opposition quickly developed, arguing that the petition was the work of brewers and distillers. After a long tedious fight, the legislature passed a bill incorporating Centennial City.

On April 30, 1897, the last day of the pre-exposition period, the financial status was gratifying. Receipts amounted to $555,609.03 and disbursements amounted to $555,183.28. This was a remarkable showing although the receipts did not include $1 of government appropriations or of the subscriptions of any county or city other than Davidson and Nashville. The money received was given, in main, by the people of Nashville.

On opening day, the streets of Nashville were thronged with a crowd estimated at 125,000 despite a steady downpour of rain. In

Exposition President John Thomas declares the exposition open.

W. A. Rogers, *Harper's Weekly, The Official History of the Tennessee Centennial Exposition*

the procession to the Centennial grounds on West End were national and state troops, ex-Confederate veterans waving the stars and bars, civic society members, a bicycle brigade, members of fraternal and benevolent orders, ladies in beautifully decorated carriages, and private citizens in carriages, on horseback, and on foot. The procession, constituting 10,000 people, stretched for eight miles. At the head of the procession rode Gen. Charles Thurman, Chief Marshall; Capt. H. C. Ward, Chief of Staff; and Col. Thomas Claiborne, Adjutant General.

As the procession approached the exposition grounds, 100 guns were fired, each representing one year of the state's history. President John W. Thomas led the flag raising and Jacob McGavock Dickinson gave the inaugural address. Later, the Honorable A. A. Taylor, of East Tennessee, gave an address "Early Days of Tennessee." His speech was followed sometime later by an address by the Hon. Edward W. Carmack, of Memphis, on the "Future of the State."

The most electrifying event of the day came in the auditorium when exposition president, John Thomas, also president of the L&N, declared the exposition officially open. At that moment, the President of the United States, pushed a button in the White House that sent an electrical impulse through Richmond and Asheville, N.C. to Nashville that put in motion the giant wheels in Machinery Hall. There was a huge applause. Immediately after the conclusion of the exercises in the auditorium, the dedication of the electrical fountain, erected by the women's department, took place. Governor Robert L. Taylor praised the woman's board before the beautiful Mrs. Van Leer Kirkman, president of the woman's board, pressed a button, which started the water flowing from the fountain. The opening day ended with a grand display of fireworks.

One of the Centennial ground's most distinctive structures was the Rialto Bridge that spanned Watauga Lake. When the West Side Race track had been there, there was only a slight depression where engineers built Lake Watauga. They used the fill from the lake to form a base for the Parthenon so that it would be somewhat elevated. The little clump of trees and shrubbery that formerly adorned the infield of the race track was left and the surrounding earth was molded to form Willow Island. Later the trees were removed and over the lake were built two bridges, the largest of which was a reproduction of the Rialto. Over the surface of the lake, Italian gondoliers rowed five picturesque gondolas brought from Venice. Also, the lake became the home for black and white swans, ducks, and geese. Facing the lake were the Negro, Agriculture, and U. S. Government Transportation buildings, all of which were temporary. The Negro Department was one of the first organized. Its department head was Mr. James C. Napier, a lawyer and a man esteemed by his community. He resigned on account of ill health and was replaced by Richard Hill, a Black school teacher. The idea of having a Negro Building was to illustrate how far the race had come since emancipation thirty years earlier. Two Black men were honored by the Negro Department—Bob Green of Belle Meade and Alfred Jackson of The Hermitage.

Every effort had been made to get President William A. McKinley to attend opening day. Although this did not work out, he and Mrs. McKinley were present on July 12 for Ohio Day. They stayed at the Maxwell House and rode in a parade of eighteen carriages from there to the Centennial grounds. His honor guard were Confederate veterans. That night McKinley's name and profile were illuminated by fireworks in a grand display.

Three of the exposition's most important days were President John Thomas Day, Nashville Day and Closing Day. It was seriously doubted that any other city in the world ever did so much with so little and with so many difficulties as did the people of Nashville in providing the major support for the exposition. Of course, the most dominating building at the exposition was the Parthenon. The idea of building, as the exposition centerpiece, an exact replica of the ancient Parthenon in Athens, Greece, was that of Major E. C. Lewis, the Centennial's director general. Inside the Parthenon were oil paintings and sculptures. The paintings were described as the most valuable works of art ever exhibited in the South. Captain William C. Smith was the architect for the Parthenon, which reminded visitors that Nashville was the Athens of the South.

One of the most unusual buildings erected at the exposition was the Memphis Building situated between the Parthenon and Watauga Lake. Memphians had reason to be proud of this building shaped in the form of a pyramid as Shelby Countians and Memphians gave more than any other city and county to the exposition except Nashville and Davidson County. The Neely Zouaves exhibited their drilling skill outside the building on Memphis Day.

I've always been impressed that the cabins in which Abraham Lincoln and Jefferson Davis were born, both in Kentucky, were both brought to Nashville on railroad flat cars and displayed at the Centennial grounds. The Centennial Exposition was, above all, a celebration of the technological progress brought by the machine age. It was one of the largest and grandest of a series of industrial expositions that became hallmarks of the new South era. Modeled after the Chicago Columbian Exposition of 1893, it also included a midway with exciting rides and exotic shows for the entertainment of families attending.

"From the top of the Seesaw they had a view of the entire Exposition by night that was simply grand beyond description."
The Official History of the Tennessee Centennial Exposition

Between May 1, 1897 and October 31, 1897, when the Centennial Celebration closed, it drew approximately 1.8 million visitors, the largest of any Southern exposition.

My grandparents visited many times as did the Weaver family of which my wife is a member. Photographs indicated that, when they visited, they wore their Sunday best clothes. There were remarkably few arrests made during the celebration, which brought favorable international attention to Nashville. A few years after the exposition closed, the grounds were converted into Centennial Park, the centerpiece of Nashville's new park system. A rebuilt Parthenon is the crowning jewel of Centennial Park today.

Farms

A Short History of the David Lipscomb Farm

The Contributor 4/10/2019

David Lipscomb moved to Davidson County with his brother, William, in 1857. They purchased a 643-acre farm in the Graves Hollow section of Bells Bend. Tolbert Fanning, whose Franklin College David had attended, sold them the land which, except for 75 acres of bottomland, was wooded. On their property David built several crude log houses.

David Lipscomb
Courtesy of Lipscomb University

In the summer of 1862, Lipscomb married Margaret "Mag" Zellner, from Maury County. She cared for her own garden, cooked, sewed, played the piano, and drew skillfully. Despite owning slaves, Lipscomb spoke out against slavery from the pulpit. There was a steamboat landing in Bells Bend named for Lipscomb. From there, corn, cord wood, cotton, grain, and lumber would be shipped to New Orleans. Brother Lipscomb began to preach from the river bank near the landing and later built a little church in the bend.

After Union forces occupied Davidson County in February 1862, David and Mag moved to Lawrenceburg, Tennessee, because it had been less touched by war. David taught school for a session at Eagle Mill in Lawrence County. After the school term ended, David and Mag, then pregnant, moved back to Bells Bend. There they lived in a log house Lipscomb built earlier on a small plateau. He enlarged it to include two rooms on either side of a dog trot. On September 23, 1863, Mag gave birth to a son, whom they named Zellner Lipscomb, for her family. Nine months later, while teething, Zellner became ill. His father tried but failed to get a physician to come to their Bells Bend home. But, as they lived in such a remote area, no physician came and Zellner died June 26, 1864.

The Lipscombs next moved from Bells Bend to a two-story house on a 110-acre dairy farm on Granny White Pike four miles from Nashville. Lipscomb purchased it for $10,600 in 1883. He kept their Bells Bend Farm which was substantially smaller than the 643-acre farm he and William bought in 1857. William had sold his interest in 1866 and David had given his nephew, David "Davey" Lipscomb Jr., part of what remained as a wedding gift in 1881.

It was not until the 1890s that David Lipscomb sold the land he had left in Bells Bend to Dr. J. H. Ward, a close friend and a coworker with Lipscomb at the Nashville Bible College that Lipscomb founded with preacher James A. Harding in 1891.

Hermitage Stud

The Contributor 3/13/2019

In the fall of 1886, some members of John Overton's family and their neighbor, Van Leer Kirkman, bought about ten standard breed trotting horses at the dispersal sale of the famous Glenview Stud in Louisville, Kentucky. After returning to Nashville, they put the horses and others they owned on a stud farm they established in 1887 which they named Hermitage Stud after Andrew Jackson's home. The syndicate

View of Hermitage Stud from Franklin Pike
Artwork of Nashville 1894–1901

consisted of Van Leer Kirkman, president; John Thompson, secretary-treasurer; May Overton, manager; and Jesse M. and Robert L. Overton, members. Robert had taken the place of his brother-in-law, Hugh Craighead.

All of the land for the stud, about 1,400 acres in all, was owned by Col. John Overton or his children: Elizabeth Overton, Jesse M. Overton, Mary McConnell "Conn" Thompson, May Overton, and Robert L. Overton. Conn lived at neighboring Glen Leven Farm with her husband, John Thompson, and their children. Kirkman lived at Oak Hill, property he had bought from Colonel Overton, while May, Robert, Jesse, and Elizabeth lived with their father at Travellers Rest.

All but one of the buildings and the training track at the Hermitage Stud were on Overton land west of Franklin Pike, mostly on the 175 acres Colonel Overton left to Conn. Her portion ran from present-day Curtiswood Lane on the north to Oak Hill property on the south, and to a creek at the "Snowden Place" on the west. The training track ran north and south near the turnpike. In the 1980s, you could still see the curve of the northern end of the track in the backyard of a home facing Harding Place a few hundred yards from

Franklin Pike. A portion of the curve at the southern end is still visible from Franklin Pike. About 100 yards from the northern end of the track there was a 24-stall training stable. In the southwest corner, there was a circular colt stable.

Most of the brood mares, usually sixty or more, were pastured in a field on the James E. Caldwell Place on the west side of Franklin Pike, about a mile or slightly more north. The stable was across the pike in the Elysian Fields track then owned by May Overton.

A month after buying the trotting horses in Kentucky, May Overton, representing the syndicate, paid John S. Clark $25,000 for the famous trotting horse Wedgewood, whose nickname was "The Iron Horse." His short racing career lasted from 1879 through 1881. In 1880, he won every race in his class in the Grand Circuit. When the Cumberland Fair and Racing Association's park opened in October 1891, the road connecting the new racecourse with the Franklin Pike was named Wedgewood in honor of the great horse.

Cumberland Driving Park lasted until 1906 when an anti-gambling law killed horse racing in Tennessee. That same year, the track became the State Fair Grounds. The Hermitage Stud weathered the 1893 depression only to close May 24, 1898, with a dispersal sale of what was advertised as the "Grandest Stud of Trotting Horses Ever in Tennessee." Part of the problem was lack of money and another part was disagreements between the partners.

By 1910, Battery Lane had been cut though the old Hermitage Stud racecourse. In 1916–17, the circular colt barn burned after being used since 1898 primarily as a cow barn. Part of the training stable was used by John and Conn Thompson to stable a saddle horse and a pony or two. The Hermitage Stud office, a square, one-room building, still stands in the backyard of a home on Curtiswood Lane.

Ferries

As Infrastructure Improved, Middle Tennessee Ferries Disappeared as a Means of Transport

The Contributor 5/12/2021

I have enjoyed a lifelong interest in Tennessee rivers and ferries. When Tennessee became a state in 1796, every river, large and small, had a ferry. Early Tennessee immigrants used Clark's Ferry to cross the Clinch River at Southwest Point. Travelers on the Natchez Trace crossed the Duck River on Gordon's Ferry. As roads and infrastructure improved, ferries began to disappear and today (2021) there are only two operating in the state, both in Middle Tennessee. Here are some of my favorite Cumberland River ferries.

Cumberland City Ferry

In 1997, F. H. "Dock" Turnbull, a licensed ferry boat pilot, told Tony Holmes, of Friendsville, Tennessee, that the Cumberland City Ferry "had experienced only five days downtime during the past seven years." The ferry, which still operates today, is owned by the Tennessee Department of Transportation and was operated in 1997 by Two Rivers Excursions, Inc. in nearby Clarksville. In 1997, it operated seven days a week from 5:30 a.m. to 6 p.m. Monday through Friday and from 6 a.m. to 6 p.m. on weekends. Vehicles registered in Stewart,

Houston and Montgomery Counties could cross all day for 75 cents and all other vehicles could cross for a dollar. The ferry, which can carry four large cars, connects the village of Cumberland City on the south side of the river with Indian Mound and Woodlawn to the north of the river. It could in 2021 carry about 100 automobiles a day. Each crossing took about five to ten minutes.

Clees Ferry

William "Bud" Hulan moved to Davidson Country from North Carolina before the Civil War. A sawmill operator and carpenter in the Bells Bend area, he ran a raft ferry across the Cumberland. It was a crude affair, operated manually. Hulan pulled it across on a cable that stretched from one bank to the other.

In the late 1860s, six Clees brothers moved to Bells Bend after living for several years in Mount Sterling, Ohio, with their widowed mother. They arrived in Davidson County collectively with $30,000, a large sum in those days. On February 3, 1869, the Clees brothers purchased 1,626 acres in Bells Bend. The brothers long wanted to build a better ferry across the river than the raft ferry Nolan operated. They first had to acquire a strip of land on the west side of the river that stretched from the riverbank to Charlotte Pike. They accomplished this in 1881 by purchasing a small wide strip of land from the Shelton family. With this done, they acquired a packet boat, which they named the *Mary Clees*, which they used as a ferry from 1877 until late 1882 when it was dismantled. That year, the Clees family moved to Pennington Bend, where they went into the soap business.

After the Clees left, the *Edgefield* operated at Bells Bend. In 1906, it or another boat was converted to a gas-powered ferry boat which could carry three cars. During the 1970s and 1980s, I periodically took my sons to ride the Clees Ferry across the Cumberland. It was fun.

When the Briley Parkway Bridge over the Cumberland opened in 1991, the Pennington Bend Ferry closed and the *Judge Hickman* moved downstream to operate at Clees Ferry. It could carry eight automobiles and served an important function into the 1990s. Today, Clees Ferry Road on the west side of the river is called Old Hickory

Boulevard. Although the ferry is gone, there is a small parking area there that has a beautiful view of the Cumberland.

Hydes Ferry

Across the Cumberland from the Beal Bosley Place in North Nashville were the homes of the Hyde brothers, Richard and Tazwell, "both clever, rich men." In the early 1840s, the Hydes established a ferry across the river. The ferry was a small, flat boat pulled on a wire by hand. Later, Richard Hyde built a larger ferry boat that carried his name. The Hydes Ferry was where the former Tennessee Central Railroad bridge is today, less than a mile downstream from the Clarksville Highway Bridge across the Cumberland.

Williamson Ferry

Williamson family members were large landowners who operated a ferry for years at McGavock Pike, beginning in 1933. Capable of carrying three cars at a time, it was named the *Edgefield* for the area west of the river which it serviced. David Lever was one of the first ferryman who operated the Williamson Ferry. The *Edgefield* was replaced by the *Judge Hickman*, built in 1952 or 1953. It could carry a total of eight cars at a time. When the Pennington Bend Bridge was completed on Briley Parkway on November 3, 1965, the *Judge Hickman* was moved downstream to the Clees Ferry site in Bells Bend. It operated there until 1991 when a construction of a bridge upstream made it obsolete.

Pennington's Ferry

This was the first ferry in Pennington Bend. It was a raft that was propelled across the river by the ferryman pulling on a rope. The ferry was located in the northwest part of the bend opposite Haysboro at a ford that was shallow enough that a wagon could be driven across the river in dry weather. Jim Pickett, a friend of mine at the Downtown Presbyterian Church, told me that, when he was a young man in the 1930s living in Pennington Bend, he once drove a wagon across the shallow Pennington ford.

The Pennington Ferry was privately owned and not generally used by the public. It was frequented by several families who lived close to the river in today's Madison. They used it to go to the one-room Methodist Church in the bend. The Craigheads and Donelsons were among the families known to have traveled to the church by this ferry.

Woods Ferry

Matthew Rhea's 1832 map of Tennessee showed at least nine ferries across the Cumberland River in Sumner County. The best known of the Sumner County ferries was Woods Ferry, south of Gallatin.

Rome Ferry

Rome was a small town in Smith County, situated at the mouth of Round Lick Creek, on the left bank of the Cumberland, eight miles west of Carthage. In 1832, it contained about 200 inhabitants, five stores, two taverns, one grocery, two tailor shops, two carpenters, one blacksmith shop, one saddlers shop, one stone mason, one cabinet shop, one shoemaker's shop, two warehouses, and one doctor.

When Rome was a thriving town, it had a ferry across the Cumberland River on what became Highway 70. The ferry continued to operate until 1992 when its last pilot died. Recently, while driving through Smith County, historian Bill Carey did a double take. He pulled over, turned the car around, and went back to see if he had imagined what he had seen. "Sure enough, it was an old, rusty ferry parked on the south bank of the Cumberland River."

Rome Ferry ca. 1980
Photo by Andy Reid III, *Wilson Living* magazine, Winter 2021

Football

Geny's All Stars

The Contributor 6/23/2021

In the 1920s, there was a Nashville amateur football league whose champion in 1927 was Oscar Geny and Sons All Stars. The team finished the year with a 12–0 record, climaxed by a 12–0 win over Louisville Bonnycastle, the defending national amateur champion.

Although hardly anyone alive can remember the Geny All Stars, the team was loaded with skilled MBA [Montgomery Bell Academy] players. Two Geny All Stars, "Chile" Hardin and Eugene "Chin" Johnson, both MBA stars, were named to the fourth annual All Southern preparatory and high school team in 1925. The next year, Robbie Worrall, a Geny All Star, and a junior at MBA, was one of two Tennesseans named to the fifth annual All Southern team. Robbie repeated as an All-Southern running back in 1927. That year, the Geny All Star's coach was Kirk Kirkpatrick, also the MBA football coach in 1925, 1926, and 1927, where his teams were undefeated. In 1928, Kirkpatrick moved to Sewanee, where he was assistant football coach. He brought with him five MBA starters, including Worrall.

Also on the 1927 Geny All Stars team was a young Cathedral athlete, Willie Geny, who would in 1935, be football captain and an All Southeastern Conference end at Vanderbilt. Oscar "Butts" Geny Jr., who had started for MBA in 1924 and 1925, was on the 1928 Geny team that defeated MBA 6–0, giving the Maroons their first defeat since 1924. If that was not enough firepower, the 1927 Geny All Stars also had future Vanderbilt coach Red Sanders as a team member.

The Geny All Stars played their home games at Sulphur Dell. The puzzle to me is that, in 1927, the Geny Coach Kirk Kirkpatrick and his star running back, Robbie Worrall, were also coaching and playing at MBA. In those days, rules for high school athletics were extremely lax. For example, MBA's star tackle, Jay Patton, didn't have any family in Nashville. Nevertheless, he started for MBA in 1927 and 1928, made possible because he lived in the attic of the new main building (today's Ball Hall).

MBA was, in 1926, 1927, and 1928, a member of the Tennessee Interscholastic Athletic Association (TIAA), among whose other members were Battle Ground Academy, Branham and Hughes Military Academy, Duncan School, and Hume-Fogg High School.

Left to right: Coach Ray Morrison, captain Willie Geny, and Pete Curley celebrate Vanderbilt's 14–6 victory over Alabama in 1935.
50 Years of Vanderbilt Football

Homes

"Acklen"

The Contributor 7/21/2016

Although Betsy Howe had a good figure and always dressed stylishly, she never married. She always said that, if she married, her husband would have to change his last name to Howe because she was not about to change her last name.

Once when Tallulah Bankhead was a guest at one of Betsy's coveted dinner parties, Betsy climbed a tree to watch and listen to the conversations of her guests, who often were an eclectic mix of actors, artists, business people, heterosexuals, homosexuals, ministers, and zoologists.

Although Betsy lived well in the city, she considered herself a farmer and had a conservatory on her three acres where she grew avocados, bananas, and tropical plants. On her lawn, she grew mushrooms. In the 1950s, she cut her lawn herself on a riding mower that she drove to neighborhood parties. She also had a horse that she kept in a stable on the back end of her property. Betsy adored her home named "Acklen." She once said, "I love that house. Besides, it's easier to keep a big house than a little one. If you mess up one room, just close the door and go in another one.'"

When a fire roared through Acklen early in the morning of June 22, 1960, Betsy, who was sleeping in her upstairs bedroom, escaped by climbing down a ladder in her nightgown. The fire left the first-floor library a charred ruin. Her dining room had its walls scorched. Betsy simply moved to her carriage house and kept on hosting the lively parties for which she was famous.

One time, Betsy said to a group of friends, "Come have dinner with me in my charcoal room. You can't stop living just because your house burns." Asked what she had for breakfast the morning of the fire, Betsy said, "I didn't have any food so I just broiled some mushrooms on toast. What could be better?" Soon Betsy moved to Washington Hall on Whitland Avenue and Acklen was razed. Today, the site is almost completely covered by a large condominium completed in 2015.

Acklen Hall, home of Betsy Howe
Collection of Ridley Wills II

Lysander McGavock's Home: "Midway"

The Contributor 1/20/2021

"Midway" was the name of Lysander McGavock's home, which he built at Good Springs in northern Williamson County in 1829. Earlier, Lysander, whose wife was the former Elizabeth Crockett, of Wythe County, Virginia, had lived near Freeland's Station where his father, David McGavock, built his brick home.

The McGavock home in Williamson County was named Midway because it was halfway between Nashville and Franklin. Good Springs later changed its name to Brentwood.

There are several theories about how Brentwood got its name. One guess is that it was named for Brentwood, Maryland. In the 1850s, the head engineer who supervised the railroad cut at Brentwood, came from Brentwood, Maryland. It is said he named the Tennessee village for his hometown.

Another theory is that Brentwood took its name from the ancestral homes of Horatio McNish in Virginia. Their names were Woodstock and Brenton. McNish lived in the Brentwood area from 1827 until the 1850s.

Lysander McGavock's Good Springs home was heavily damaged by a fire in the mid 1840s and was replaced in 1846 by the brick home that is now the clubhouse of the Brentwood Country Club. Nashville mayor John Cooper and his brother Jim Cooper, our long-time congressman, are McGavock descendants, as I am.

"Midway," Lysander McGavock's home
Historic Brentwood

"Peach Blossom"

The Contributor 2/29/2016

Joseph Erwin was nearly forty years old when he moved to Davidson County with his wife, Lavinia, his parents, and seven children. By 1805, he owned 1,000 acres of good bottomland. There, he built on the road from Cockrill Spring to Richland Creek one of the first brick houses in Davidson County. The bricks were manufactured on his premises, and the timber cut from his hardwood trees. Behind the house, with its great columns and overhanging porch, were the

Peach
Blossom,
ca. 1968
Collection of
Tim Douglas

slave quarters just twenty-five feet away, and nearby a smokehouse. For water, there was a cistern into which rainwater from the roof was piped.

Erwin's wealth came quickly in the little town of Nashville that was booming. He made his money from the cotton, tobacco, corn, and wheat he grew and from Thoroughbreds he raced. Annually, Erwin took his cotton down the Cumberland, Ohio, and Mississippi rivers to the market in New Orleans. There, he bought supplies for his plantation, which had, as its boundaries from today's 32nd Avenue on West End to where Montgomery Bell Academy is today. The plantation fronted on today's West End between 3704 and 3708. It extended east to today's Woodlawn Drive.

Erwin also bought luxuries in New Orleans for his house that he named "Peach Blossom" because of his peach orchard. The Erwins had three daughters. One married Col. Andrew Hynes, the second became the bride of William Blount Robertson, brother of Dr. Felix Robertson. The third, Jane, married Charles Henry Dickinson II, a young sportsman and farmer, who was killed in a duel with Andrew Jackson.

"Polk Place"

The Contributor 2/22/2016

This view of "Polk Place" was taken from Vine Street (Seventh Avenue North). To the right of the house, built by Felix Grundy between 1818 and 1820, was the tomb of James K. Polk, who purchased Grundy Hill while president as his and Mrs. Polk's retirement home.

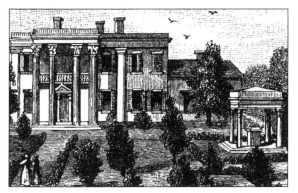

When built by Grundy, the width of the house was a little more than seventy-four feet. The walls were made of red brick, the steps and windowsills of stone, and the roof of cedar shingles. The window shutters were painted dark green. President Polk made extensive alterations to the house to convert it into the then-popular Neo-Grecian style. James M. Hughes did the renovation. While an excellent builder, Hughes was not a good architect. When he finished, all that was left of Grundy Hill was the "side of the house from the doorway north."

President Polk only lived in Polk Place for fifty-three days, dying there June 15, 1849. In his will, he left the house to his wife for her lifetime. His will stated that, on her death, the historic home would be left in trust to the State of Tennessee. However, collateral descendants broke the will and sold Polk Place to a developer, J. Craig McClanahan. He dismantled Nashville's most historic house in 1901 and built Polk Flats apartments on the site.

Two years after Mrs. Polk's death, the tomb containing her body and that of President Polk was moved to the east side of the Capitol grounds, where it stands today. A hotel and the old Ben West Public

Library are two of the buildings that now stand on the site. McClanahan gave the property on which the library was built to the city.

"Terrace Place" Once a Family Home

The Contributor 1/16/2017

"Terrace Place" was built on Church Street by Nashville business magnate Edmund W. "King" Cole. The construction was completed before he married his second wife, Anna Russell, of Augusta, Georgia, on Christmas Eve of 1872. Friends and acquaintances of Anna in Augusta considered her the "Pride of Georgia" and the most beautiful woman in the state. Consequently, they were dismayed that she would move to Nashville after falling in love with a rich Tennessee widower with five children from his first marriage.

Anna was impressed when she first saw her magnificent home in Nashville. Before walking in, E. W. showed her their carved initials, "C and R," above the front door. Anna quickly learned that Sarah Childress Polk, the sixty-nine-year-old widow of James K. Polk, was her next-door neighbor on the east. E. W. undoubtedly

Terrace Place, for twenty years the home of Anna Russell Cole and her husband, Nashville businessman Edmund Cole

alerted Anna to the fact that, except for Mrs. Polk's visits to her home-town of Murfreesboro and regularly attending First Presbyterian Church a few blocks away, she did not go out, did not socialize, and did not return visits. Unquestionably, the Coles called on her.

Anna was a good stepmother and mother to her own two children: Whiteford, born in 1874, and Anna Russell, born in 1879, at Terrace Place. She and E. W. lived there for twenty years. Then Mr. Cole sold the house and built an even grander Colonial-style home, called "Colemere," seven miles from town on Murfreesboro Pike.

The Coles moved from their home on Church Street because the area was rapidly becoming commercial. Mrs. Polk had just died and E. W. suspected that the part of her block-square property facing Church Street would soon be developed commercially. On the other side of Terrace Place, at the northeast corner of Church and Spruce streets, the I. C. Nicholson house, which had operated as a high-class boarding house since 1860, was replaced in the early 1890s by a six-story hotel. (It would be renamed "The Tulane.")

As E. W. knew, Terrace Place was more valuable as commercial property than as residential. He sold his palatial mansion to the Southern Baptist Sunday School Board, which occupied it until the need for additional space led them to move their headquarters to their new four-story Frost Building at 161 Eighth Ave. North. Not many years later, Terrace Place was replaced by a five-story Doctors' Building designed by Edward E. Daugherty, best-known in Nashville for designing the new Nashville Golf and Country (Belle Meade Country Club) clubhouse.

"West Meade"

The Contributor 4/4/2016

In 1883, Gen. William G. Harding, having suffered a stroke and speaking only with great difficulty, divided his farm, "Belle Meade," between his two daughters, Selene and Mary Elizabeth, and their husbands, Gen. William H. Jackson, and U. S. Senator Howell E. Jackson. Because his son-in-law, William H. Jackson, had assisted him in managing Belle Meade since Billy married Selene in 1868, Gen. Harding gave them the western part of the plantation that included the house, the deer park, and the land south of Harding Road and east of the Lower Franklin Pike (today's Page Road)—in all 2,167 acres. He gave Mary Elizabeth and Howell the land north of Harding Road and west of the Lower Franklin Pike, including the High Pasture (part of today's Percy Warner Park). Their property included 2,600 acres. Gen. Harding gave his son, John Harding Jr., all his Thoroughbred horses, including 80-odd mares, 4 stallions, and 49 colts and fillies.

West Meade was the home of Mary Elizabeth Harding Jackson and Justice Howell E. Jackson.   Collection of Ridley Wills II

In 1882, Howell no longer felt strong ties to Jackson, Tennessee, because his father, who had been a force there since 1840, died in 1879. Accordingly, Howell and Mary Elizabeth moved to Davidson County and began fixing up the old Tealey Place, which they moved into in 1883. When W. W. Tealey died in 1881, the Jacksons purchased his house and property that stretched west to the base of Nine Mile Hill.

Three years later, Howell and Mary completed "West Meade" on the site of the Tealey house. West Meade was one mile southwest of Belle Meade, and seven miles from Nashville. The splendid new house cost $12,800 while the smokehouse cost $750. West Meade was completed soon after Jackson resigned as U.S. Senator to accept his appointment by President Grover Cleveland as judge of the Sixth Circuit Court of Appeal.

In 1892, after his defeat by Grover Cleveland in the 1892 presidential election, but before his term expired early in 1893, President Benjamin Harrison had an opportunity to fill an open position on the Supreme Court. Despite the fact that Howell Jackson was a Democrat, a friend of President Cleveland, a Southerner, and a former Confederate, Harrison submitted his name to the Senate for consideration. Jackson was quickly confirmed and took his seat on March 4, 1893. This non-partisan action by President Harrison would never happen in the highly partisan world of today.

After Associate Justice Jackson started suffering from severe lung problems, he and his wife decided to rent an elegant five-bedroom house named "Southside Villa" outside Thomasville, Georgia, where the pine-scented air was supposed to alleviate respiratory problems. Jackson's last public act was his most courageous. In March 1895, he returned to Washington to cast his vote on the *Pollock v. Farmers' Loan and Trust Company* case. The other eight judges were evenly divided on whether or not a Federal Income Tax was constitutional. Jackson was in favor of the tax. Unexpectedly, one of the justices changed his mind and, by a vote of five to four, the act was held unconstitutional. Jackson's delivery of his opinion displayed masterful reasoning showing that his mind was as bright as his body was weak. He died of tuberculosis on August 8, 1895, at age sixty-three. His widow, Mary Harding, continued to live at West Meade until her death in 1913.

In her will, Mrs. Jackson left West Meade to her three children, Elizabeth Jackson Buckner, Louise Jackson McAlister, and Harding Alexander Jackson. For a year or two, Mrs. Jackson's daughter, Louise, her husband, Hill McAlister, and their young daughters, Louise and Laura, lived at West Meade. At different times, other family members lived there, including a granddaughter, Elizabeth Buckner, after her marriage to John Keith Maddin in 1922.

It was not until 1944 that the Jackson descendants sold West Meade to a group of investors headed by E. A. Wortham and Brownlee O. Currey. The two businessmen paid $175,000 for the property (1,750 acres) and announced plans to cut up the land into small tracts, after selling the house and fifty acres to Mrs. Ronald Voss. The small farms have long since disappeared in favor of post–World War II largely ranch-style homes that dominate today's West Meade section of Nashville.

Hand-drawn map of 227-acre Island Track, where the Peyton Stakes horse race was held

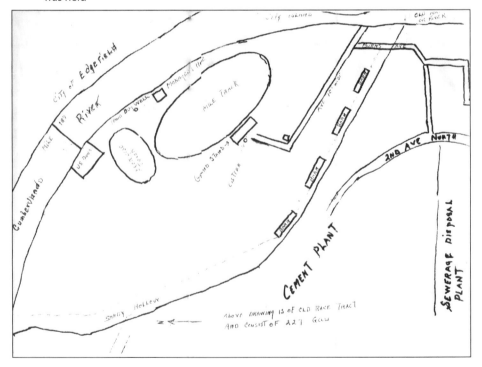

Horse Races

Peyton Stakes

The Contributor 3/17/2021

In an earlier "Nashville History Corner" article, I wrote about the Grassland International Steeplechases held in Sumner County in 1930 and 1931. An even more remarkable race took place on a glorious day, October 10, 1843, when the richest horse race ever run anywhere in the world took place at the Nashville Race Course (Burns Island Track) on the south bank of the Cumberland River. This was the $35,000 Peyton Stakes, which far eclipsed the value of any race in Europe or North America for quite a few years. For example, the famous Derby at Epson was worth $21,250 in 1843.

The idea of having the Peyton Stakes in Nashville was that of Balie Peyton, of Gallatin. He thought big. The starting fee was $5,000 and the distance was sixteen miles. The 1840s was the heyday of long races. Each heat was to be four miles. If a different horse won each of the first three heats, there would be a fourth heat to determine the winner. Horses from nine states—Alabama, Kentucky, Louisiana, North and South Carolina, Maryland, Mississippi, Tennessee, and Virginia— were nominated to run.

The *Spirit of the Times* sent a reporter, whose pen name was "Rover," to cover the event. He was complimentary of Nashville, which he described as "one of the most picturesque and thriving of the cities

89

of the west." The only negative was the condition of the track which was heavy with sticky mud after two days of incessant rain.

The big betting was on Herald, owned by Col. Wade Hampton, of South Carolina. However, the first heat was won by a chestnut colt by Imp. Skylark, from Lilac by Imp. Leviathan, owned by the Hon. Alex Barrow of Louisiana. Herald came back to win the second heat. In the third heat, Herald had the lead for much of the race. However, on the final turn, a horse named Glumdalclitch was forced by his jockey, Barney Palmer, to swing wide and avoid the deepest mud. The filly responded by beating Herald home by about a length, running the 12th mile in 1:58.

In the tie-breaking fourth heat, Barney Palmer repeated his tactic that had worked so well in the third heat, "turning on the heat at the last quarter stretch of the fourth mile, to beat Herald again by almost a length." Col. Balie Peyton's Great Western was never in contention. Track owner Lysander McGavock was pleased.

The winner, Glumdalclitch, was a powerful mare, standing about 19½ hands. In honor of the stakes, her owner renamed her "Peytona." She went on to win many more races.

The Peyton Stakes was the high point of the Island Track or any other track around Nashville. After four years of inactivity during the Civil War, racing resumed at the Island Track each spring and fall. The track, then owned by Michael Burns, began to suffer for lack of maintenance and the lack of a mule car line to the track. The last race there was on May 7, 1884.

Courtesy of *The Contributor*

The Southern Grassland Hunt and Racing Foundation

The Contributor 3/3/2021

This private hunting park and equestrian sports center was stunning. Prior to this venture in 1930, no private preserve had ever been laid out in the United States. Grasslands in Sumner County was conceived by a small but wealthy group of foxhunters in the autumn of 1929. Mason Houghland and Rogers Caldwell of Nashville and John M. Branham of Gallatin were three of the founding members. All were avid foxhunters. They invited Joseph B. Thomas, a famous eastern breeder of foxhounds, to Nashville. Impressed with the lay of the land, Thomas was especially ecstatic about the farmland that surrounded Branham's home, Foxland Hall, near Gallatin. Thomas and his local hosts identified twenty-eight square miles of farmland, with Foxland Hall near its center, as a potential sportsman's park. The land was bordered by the Cumberland River on the south, Woods Ferry Pike on the east, Highway 31-E, a railroad and an electric streetcar line on the north, and Drakes Creek on the west.

The well-watered site with groves of magnificent shade trees seemed perfect for foxhunting, steeplechasing, polo, and other outdoor events. Two other like-minded sportsmen of the hunt and chase—Arnold Hanger of Richmond, Kentucky, and Julius Fleishmann Jr. of Cincinnati—joined the development group and organized a corporation to acquire the land, and another corporation to operate sporting events.

On October 23, 1929, the State of Tennessee issued a charter of incorporation to the Sumner County Land Company, Inc. Thomas, Branham, Caldwell, Fleishmann, and Houghland then established the Southern Grasslands Hunt and Racing Foundation. Each man put up $10,000 to pay for memberships. Offering premium prices, the local farm owners signed up quickly to sell their land to the Land Company. Soon, the land company controlled twenty-eight square miles of land. Included in the purchase was the historic 600-acre Fairview Farm.

In December 1929, the founders distributed a sixteen-page prospectus in hopes of attracting more members, as only about $500,000 had been paid by subscribers. Already, a house on 31-A was converted into an inn called Race Horse Tavern and out-buildings were constructed and landscaping accomplished. Before fences were put in place, they were dipped in crude oil which gave them a nice yellow color. The work crew in February totaled two hundred men, many of whom were building stables for three hundred horses and kennels for the dogs.

In the spring three race courses were laid out. They were located "in a beautiful lowland" easily seen from higher ground. Outsiders, wealthy sportsmen, all multi-millionaires, took memberships but never as many as were needed. A strict dress code was adopted, with members wearing scarlet coats. The hunt staff wore yellow coats with scarlet colors. Although there were lots of gray foxes on the purchased farmland, more red foxes were needed. In the spring, a shipment of red foxes arrived at the L&N station in Gallatin. Charles Carter came on board as the huntsman at Grassmere.

With the steeplechase course progressing nicely, the inaugural steeplechase was scheduled for May 19, 1930. On race day, members of Grasslands and their guests gathered on the veranda and lawn of Foxland Hall to watch it. The event was hoped to win support from prominent sports people across the country. A Nashville newspaper bragged that the event was "held in a setting never before equaled for color and brilliance in either the social or sporting history of Nashville." On a muddy course, Red Gold, owned and ridden by Byron Hilliard of Louisville won the inaugural event.

Promotion quickly started for the first International Steeplechase. By November 3, Grasslands had received nine entries and it was hoped that there would be twenty before the entry deadline of December 1. Four were English horses, the rest American. By December 1, there were twenty-four entries for the December 6 event. This was a welcome diversion from the Depression, which caused Rogers Caldwell to lose $2 million a day during one week. On Friday night, a Bal Poudre (powdered wig ball) held at Fairview was the social highlight of the

Grasslands International Steeplechase, 1931
A Pictorial History of Sumner County, Tennessee

weekend. There was also a fox hunt. On Saturday, an unusually cold one, Alligator was first to cross the finish line.

The race was successful in that the course was in a class with Aintree Racecourse in England. European horses participated in the event, and there was a good attendance. What was not successful was that new member recruiting lagged. The *Tennessean* reported that the race was successful and that its running in future years was assured. That turned out to be wrong. With lagging financial support, the Southern Grasslands Hunt and Racing Foundation restructured itself and persuaded creditors to give the foundation more time to pay its notes. None of this would work, however, unless they got new members. Prospective members were invited to visit Grasslands. A new category of membership was introduced with significantly smaller initiation fees and annual dues of only $15.

There were two competing steeplechase events in America in 1931. One was the Prince of Wales Gold Cup Race near Lexington on November 12. It was followed by the Piedmont Hunt Race on November 17 in Upperville, Virginia. The Grassland owners viewed both as prep races for Grasslands. The second Grasslands International Steeplechase was held December 5, 1931, over the most grueling race course in America. Again, as in 1930, the chase was preceded by fox hunting. The night before the race, four hundred guests attended a costume ball at Fairview. The women wore wigs and evening gowns while the gentlemen wore formal hunting attire. Until midnight, everyone wore masks. There were also trap shoots and pigeon shoots with national champions competing. Thirteen horses competed in the second international Steeplechase at Grasslands. Glangesis, owned by Richard K. Mellon, won with a time 10 minutes and 14 seconds better than the winning time in 1930. No horses were injured and only two jockeys suffered injuries that required medical treatment. The 1931 race was a great show but the financial results were truly disappointing. Foundation members noticed that about 3,000 of the 10,000 who witnessed the race did so outside the grounds of Grasslands and didn't pay anything. Despite the monetary problems, President Arnold Hanger announced that the third Grasslands International Steeplechase would be held December 3, 1932.

Despite restructuring the memberships again, this time to attract more Nashvillians, problems persisted. John Hay Whitney was asked to purchase the real estate of the Sumner County Land Association and lease it back to Grasslands. This didn't work and Gallatin merchants filed suit to recover money owed them. In truth, the Grassland Company was insolvent. Frantic efforts by the Grassland owners to survive brought little sympathy from Nashvillians who were preoccupied with dealing with the Depression.

On October 17 and 18, the Grassland trustees sold sixty-two tracts of property, primarily to previous owners of the land. Many farmers found their land in better shape than when they earlier owned it, with better fencing and gates. The brush jumps on the course withered and rotted. The kennels and barns, without maintenance, slowly deteriorated and commercial and residential development resulted in their demolition. Today, the only visual reminder of Grasslands is the original water tower which stands near where the Race Horse Tavern once stood. The great effort to transplant English sports culture to Middle Tennessee lasted twenty-nine months. Grassland's survival that long was more than a minor achievement.

Hotels

Andrew Jackson Hotel

The Contributor 7/27/2015

When the Andrew Jackson Hotel opened in August 1925, it was, for a few weeks, the largest hotel in the state with 400 rooms. The Andrew Jackson was soon eclipsed in size by the Peabody Hotel in Memphis which had 625 rooms.

The Andrew Jackson, located on the east side of Memorial Square at the corner of Sixth Avenue North and Deaderick Street, was one block away from its fiercest competitor, The Hermitage Hotel, which opened in 1910. Most of the great political campaigns between the two factions of the Democratic Party in Tennessee were waged from these two, first-class hotels.

The first Democratic campaign headquartered at the Andrew Jackson and Hermitage Hotels was the gubernatorial race in 1926 between Hill McAllister and Austin Peay. For the ensuing half century, campaign strategy was hammered out in smoke-filled rooms in both hotels.

Adorning the front of the Andrew Jackson during political races were huge posters promoting the campaigns of Austin Peay, Henry H. Horton, Cordell Hull, Gordon Browning, Albert Gore, and Estes Kefauver. Senator Gore always had a special fondness for the Andrew Jackson because it was in the coffee shop there that he met his wife, the former Pauline Lafon, who was a waitress there working her way through law school. Gore had come in for a cup of coffee before driving home to Carthage, Tennessee.

The greatest triumph of the Andrew Jackson group came in 1948. That was the year when Kefauver and Browning at last broke the power of the state-wide political machine controlled by Edward H. "Boss" Crump, who was known as the "red snapper of Tennessee politics."

The twelve-story Andrew Jackson Hotel was demolished on June 13, 1971, to make way for the Tennessee Performing Arts Center and the James K. Polk State Office Building, completed in 1976.

A postcard of the Andrew Jackson Hotel— Often huge posters hung at the front of the hotel during campaigns for politicians, including Austin Peay, Henry H. Horton, Cordell Hull, and other Democrats.
Collection of Ridley Wills II

Good Roads Killed the Sedberry Hotel

The Contributor 1/8/2020

The last time I was in McMinnville, I forgot to look for the old three-story, red-brick Sedberry Hotel, long closed, to see if it was still standing. When I was a teenager in the years immediately following World War II, I remember my grandmother, Jessie Ely (Mrs. Ridley) Wills, taking me to the Sedberry Hotel on a Sunday for dinner. Her chauffeur, Lemuel Wilson, drove us in a Packard on U.S. 70 South from Nashville through Murfreesboro, and Woodbury to McMinnville. There we saw a lot of cars parked close to the hotel. When we went inside to the dining room, we found that it was run by Miss Connie Sedberry, while her sister Erbye ran the rest of the 50-room hotel. They inherited the place and its famous restaurant in 1931 when their mother died. Mrs. Sedberry had owned the hotel and run it and the restaurant from 1914 when she bought it for it for $15,000 until her death.

Mrs. Sedberry, with help from her young daughters and faithful cooks, established the restaurant's great reputation. Initially, her clients were mostly drummers (traveling salesmen), who traveled by two-horse wagons *and* usually stayed for three or four weeks. Breakfast in the early days had to be served at 4:55 a.m. to enable guests to catch the Tullahoma train. Pork chops and pancakes were breakfast favorites.

Sedberry Hotel,
McMinnville, Tennessee

For a while, the Sedberry was strategically located on the north-south route from Nashville to Chattanooga and on the east-west route from Knoxville to Memphis. Those years were the Sedberry's heydays. Miss Connie gave special attention to what she called "the Congressional crowd." Among the famous politicians to eat and stay at the Sedberry were the John Nance Garners, who always stayed in room 135; the Alben Barkleys of Kentucky; Huey Long, whom Miss Connie thought was the "kindest man"; Cordell Hull; and John Connally. Texas Representative Sam Rayburn spent part of his honeymoon there.

The non-political crowd was also impressive and diverse. Hedda Hopper came, as did Al Capone one Sunday before Thanksgiving. John Dillinger visited once, as did the J. Pierpont Morgans. One day, Babe Ruth, having missed his plane in Nashville, stopped while hurrying by car to Knoxville to catch a New York train. As he ran out the front door, clutching a piece of pecan pie, he was said to have shouted over his shoulder: "I'm going to make a home run out of this." After Duncan Hines, the culinary critic, visited, he wrote in his *Adventures in Good Eating,* that "Dinner at the Sedberry is a knockout."

Once, during the Middle Tennessee maneuvers in 1943, five generals were eating at the Sedberry at the same time. My guess is that when I went with my grandmother we had a fried chicken dinner with stuffed baked squash, a fancy salad and corn sticks, followed by a piece of pecan pie for dessert. We just as easily could have had a country ham dinner with homemade lemon ice cream for dessert. Miss Connie usually served six different meats on Sundays.

Better roads were the biggest factor in the decline and closure of the Sedberry. A shorter, smoother U.S. 70 North that went through Lebanon and Cookeville well north of McMinnville may have drained off enough travelers to cause Tennessee to lose perhaps its greatest small-town restaurant.

Richardsonian Romanesque Utopia Hotel

The Contributor 10/6/2014

The Utopia Hotel, 206 Fourth Avenue North, is a narrow, six-story building whose façade is constructed in the Romanesque Revival style. It was built in 1890, when Nashville was the state's largest city. The hotel is distinguished by its slightly projecting three-story bay, its "rich detailing of carved, foliated forms, and its variety of windows."

In the 1892 City Directory, the hotel's advertisement read "European Hotel and Restaurant, Saloon, Cigars, and Tobacco."

The first manager of the Utopia was Ike Johnson, who shortly thereafter left to manage the Southern Turf deeper in the Men's Quarter on Fourth Avenue North. He gained for the Southern Turf a national reputation as a place where men could eat, drink, and gamble without police interference.

William P. Polston was the Utopia's second manager. He was known for his generosity to the poor by hosting a "bread line" and by providing Christmas dinners to the homeless. Polston managed the hotel until 1910, a year before he died.

Utopia Hotel, Nashville
Nyttend, 2014, Wikimedia Commons

The next owner of the Utopia changed its name to the Bismarck Hotel and Café. This lasted until 1920 when the name reverted to the Utopia. The hotel closed in 1933 during the Depression and over the next number of decades became the home of a barber shop, a dry-cleaning operation, and an office. The hotel's dining room, on the first floor, was greatly modified to become the dry-cleaning business. Accordingly, most of the detail there was lost. Fortunately, much detail remains on the upper floors. The woodwork is also largely intact on the upper floors that are only twenty-five feet wide. Still there are twenty-five immense, paneled sliding doors, massive moldings and balustrades. On the upper floors a hallway runs the length of the building, which is 174 feet long.

In the basement there is a restaurant that opens onto Printers Alley, another entertainment district.

Libraries

Nashville's Andrew Carnegie Library

The Contributor 6/8/2015

A ndrew Carnegie once wrote "I believe that building libraries out-ranks any other one thing that a community can do to benefit its people." In 1901, Carnegie sold his huge steel enterprise for $480 million, making him the second wealthiest man in America. Soon, he began supporting a free library system across North America.

In 1917, Carnegie had funded the construction of at least 1,689 free public libraries in the United States and another 830 throughout the English-speaking world. Earlier in October 1901, Carnegie offered the City of Nashville $100,000 for a new public library. The city accepted the offer and held a national competition for an architect,

Postcard of Nashville's Andrew Carnegie Library, which opened in the summer of 1904
Collection of Ridley Wills II

ultimately selecting New York architect Albert Randolph Ross, who submitted a modern Beaux Arts design.

The cornerstone for the new library at the southeast corner of Spruce and Union streets was laid April 27, 1903. The library opened in the summer of 1904. The Carnegie Library stood until 1963 when it was razed and replaced by the Ben West Public Library, which was operational for thirty-eight years.

[2022 Note: The Carnegie Library at Spruce and Union streets was the first of four public libraries in Nashville funded by Andrew Carnegie. The second was a Carnegie Library on the Fisk University campus that opened in 1909 and is no longer a library. The third is the North Nashville Carnegie Library at 101 Monroe Street. Opened in 1915, it remains open today. The last of the Carnegie Libraries in Nashville is the East Branch Carnegie Library, which opened in 1919 at 206 Gallatin Pike. It is still functioning as a public library today.]

Ben West Library

The Contributor 6/8/2015

When the new building of the Public Library of Nashville and Davidson County, named for Mayor Ben West, opened in January 1966, a Nashville Room emerged complete with red carpet, old books, and Nashville memorabilia. The books were those formerly found in the Tennessean Collection in the old Carnegie Library, which was on the same spot as the Ben West Library. For many years, the Nashville Room was run by the very capable Mary Glen Hearne, librarian.

The Ben West Public Library, after serving the city for thirty-eight years, closed in 2001 when the new Public Library of Nashville and Davidson County opened at 615 Church Street.

Night Riders

Night Riders in the Tobacco Patch

The Contributor 10/9/2019

In the early 1890s, dark-fired tobacco was selling in Adams, Clarksville, and Springfield, Tennessee, and Guthrie, Kentucky for 2, 3, or 4 cents per pound. The cost of raising one acre was $42, but the sale of one acre yielded only $28. In 1904, the Planter's Protective Tobacco Association of Kentucky, Tennessee, and Virginia was organized to bring farmers, who were becoming desperate, an equitable price for tobacco. The association held its first meeting in Guthrie in 1907. Approximately 5,000 people, probably triple the population of the town, were present. President of the association was Charles Fort, whose great-great-grandfather, Elias Fort, had migrated from Edgecombe County, North Carolina around 1790 to Tennessee County, North Carolina.

In 1830, Fort's grandson, Joel Battle Fort, built a large, two-story Greek Revival home named "Meridian Hill." His mansion was in what became known as the Black Patch tobacco region and was representative of the wealthy tobacco growers' plantation homes. When Fort died in 1867, he left Meridian Hill to his daughter, Susannah Fort Ligon. A year later, she sold the home to her brother, Josiah William Fort, whose wife was Eliza Dancy Fort. They moved to Meridian Hill in Robertson County, Tennessee, northwest of Springfield at Sadlersville, where Josiah followed in his father's footsteps by continuing to raise tobacco. He also was a Baptist preacher and judge. Josiah's third son, Charles, became the next master of Meridian Hill.

Attempts to break the planter's Protective Tobacco Association were led by the American Tobacco Company and the Italian firm, Regie. J. B. Duke, who controlled the American Tobacco Company, paid higher prices for the dark-fire tobacco to a group called the "Hillbillies" that declined to join the Planters Protective Tobacco Association. Duke's idea was to dissuade farmers from supporting the association. During the most heated period of controversy, Fort stood firmly with the association. He was threatened when he received a letter that read, "Dear Sir, we give you ten days to withdraw from the Planter's Protective Association as president or you had better order a bodyguard." In response, Fort issued a statement that read, "I shall never resign the office of president until the people who elected me request it." The affair ended without incident.

In 1906, one wing of the association began vigilante activities. Thirty-one men were present when this group first met in Stainback School. They called themselves "The Possum Hunters." Violence broke out when warehouses in nearby Adams and Clarksville were burned as were numerous privately-owned tobacco barns. Private individuals, including ex-sheriff Ben Sory, were also threatened. Because the warehouses and barns were burned at night, people in the area called those who did this "The Night Riders."

The Night Riders' activities reached a climax in 1907 with raids on the homes and barns of L. W. Lawrence and G. W. Fletcher. One

Kentucky tobacco barn

Night Rider was killed and several others recognized. Not long afterward, "Trust Buster" Teddy Roosevelt, during his term as President of the United States, ordered a suit to be brought against the American Tobacco Company and other monopolies. This anti-trust action resulted in American Tobacco Company being broken up into several still major groups in 1911. Tobacco prices began to steadily rise and the Night Riders were disbanded.

The Night Riders of Reelfoot Lake

The Contributor 11/27/2019

In the October 9, 2019 issue of *The Contributor*, I wrote about Night Riders in Robertson County, who, in 1907, burned private barns and tobacco warehouses to protest the monopoly that the American Tobacco Company had that prevented tobacco growers from receiving equitable prices.

In 1908, there was another group of Night Riders—this time in Lake and Obion counties. This Night Rider episode resulted from a dispute over the title to Reelfoot Lake and the surrounding land.

Created by the violent earthquake of 1811–12, the lake, filled with fish, supplemented the diets and incomes of perhaps a majority of families living in the vicinity. Although claims on the land existed prior to the earthquake, the local population considered the lake public domain. When the West Tennessee Land Company purchased old claims and began preparations to drain at least part of the lake and convert it into cotton land, the mostly poor residents of Obion and Lake counties were, rightfully so, furious.

On the night of October 19, 1908, after several weeks of increasing violence, masked riders kidnapped two officers of the West Tennessee Land Company, R. Z. Taylor and Quinton Rankin, from Ward's Hotel in Walnut Log, Tennessee. The Night Riders murdered Rankin, but Taylor managed to escape by hiding in a swamp under a cypress log. He was found twenty-four hours later, disoriented and wandering in the swamp. Gov. Malcolm Patterson took charge of the situation and arrived at Reelfoot with the Tennessee National Guard. By the end of October, nearly 100 suspects had been arrested and were incarcerated in a make-shift camp set up by the National Guard. Their treatment by the Guard was harsh and two of the prisoners died while awaiting trial. Eventually, six men were convicted of murdering Quinton Rankin and sentenced to death. In 1909, the Tennessee Supreme Court overturned their convictions. Public opinion heavily supported the plight of the Reelfoot Lake people. As a result, the State of Tennessee acquired title to the lake in 1914, ending the threat of private ownership. In 1925, the state purchased land surrounding the lake and established the Reelfoot Lake Park and Fish and Game Preserve.

From the 1960s to the 1980s, the state made a series of improvements, including a visitor's center, a museum, lodge, restaurant, and an airplane landing strip. Today, Reelfoot Lake attracts thousands of fishermen, duck hunters, and nature lovers, who particularly enjoy seeing the American bald eagles, who spend their winter months there.

Walnutlog, Tennessee—the tree where Capt. Quinton Rankin was hung and the point where Col. R. Z. Taylor plunged in the slough
Collection of Ridley Wills II

Parks/Zoos

Belle Meade Deer Park

The Contributor 9/26/2016

William Giles Harding married Selena McNairy, the seventeen-year-old daughter of Mr. and Mrs. Nathaniel McNairy, on November 19, 1829. The young couple started their married life on his father's Stones River Plantation. Their farm was a 579-acre tract that John Harding had purchased in 1827. Because his land contained both woods and fields, game abounded. In 1833 or 1834, William Giles and his father took five deer from the farm in McSpadden's Bend to Belle Meade where Mr. Harding established a deer park where the deer would be safe and could breed. In time, the herd grew to several hundred and the deer park became a landmark and an unofficial park for Davidson County.

One of the earliest accounts of the deer park was published in 1854. It said that the park "contained 14 buffalo and as many as 200 deer." Harding later introduced elk from the Northwest to the park and eventually imported Indian water-oxen for his menagerie.

In 1858, the *Republican Banner and Nashville Whig* contained an article on a picnic at the deer park. The scribe wrote, "Everybody knows something of this delightful spot." He added that the park's natural beauties were unrivaled particularly to "one who spends his days and nights in a dusty city." Park visitors sometimes brought a complete band with them, but, more frequently, only a violin or banjo. As the number of visitors to the park increased, it became increasingly difficult to control them. To counter this, Mrs. Elizabeth Harding (William Giles Harding's second wife after Selena died) had her slave Bob Green put up a sign at the front gate saying the park was closed on Sundays. Visitors still came to the house Sunday afternoons and begged permission to come in, saying that Sunday was the only time they could visit. Mrs. Harding usually relented.

During the Federal occupation of Nashville, Union soldiers wanted to see the park. Elizabeth Harding in a May 15, 1862, letter to her husband William Giles Harding (then a political prisoner at Fort Mackinac, Michigan) said, "Some Federals have just called to go in the park and Mr. Hague [William Hague, Belle Meade stock manager] has gone out to escort them; I like him to be about on such occasions; he does 'the honors' to the best of his ability, and they seem satisfied with his quaker ways." Less than four months later, marauding Federal soldiers killed 60 of the 100 deer and all but one of the 12 or 14 buffalo in the deer park.

After the Civil War, a good many of the former slaves chose to stay at Belle Meade, where they worked for General Harding under a contract system. One of the rules was that the laborers and their families were not allowed to shoot or trap partridges, mockingbirds, or squirrels in the deer park. With the loss of many animals from the deer park during the war, Gen. Harding and his son-in-law, Gen. William H. Jackson, gradually restocked the herd. As was the case before the Civil War, the 425-acre deer park was not cultivated. When guests came to Belle Meade, they invariably either rode or walked throughout the park to see the deer that were confined by the stone wall that surrounded it. Because the deer could easily jump the wall, wood slates were built on top of the walls to make the enclosure twelve feet high.

Historian George Bancroft visited Nashville in April 1887 to examine the papers of deceased President James K. Polk. On the last day of his visit, he and his German valet Hermann and a committee of the Tennessee Historical Society drove out to Belle Meade. Gen. William H. Jackson and Judge Howell E. Jackson greeted them on the front lawn. After thirty minutes of conversation, Gen. Jackson invited Bancroft and his party to drive through the deer park. A half-dozen horses were quickly saddled and brought to the front door, along with several carriages for the eighty-five-year-old Bancroft and others. A Nashville reporter, who accompanied the group, noticed that Hermann seemed "as unexcitable and immovable as stone until taken through the park." However, when "a drove of perhaps 200 deer dashed by, he said, in an excited voice 'Well, did you ever see anything like that?' Bancroft's voice trembled when he responded, 'Never in my life.'"

President Grover Cleveland and his wife viewing the deer at Belle Meade
Drawing by Gilbert Gaul, *Harper's Weekly*, 1887

President Grover Cleveland and his wife visited Belle Meade in October 1887. They too visited the deer park where Bob Green and some of his helpers corralled the deer and drove them past the chief executive. The president turned to Gen. Jackson and said, "That was a splendid sight, General. It made my nerves tingle. I never saw such an exhibition before."

At the Tennessee Centennial Celebration in 1897, Gen. Jackson admired a large buck elk named Ben Yaka, in the midway. The elk stood nearly 16 hands high and weighed as much as a horse. Jackson bought Ben Yaka and its mate Nellie, and had them brought to his deer park when the celebration ended. Renamed Tommy, the huge elk became the park's most notorious resident. Jackson and park visitors realized that Tommy was anything but shy. One spring, he was particularly rambunctious and turned over a buggy. On another occasion, two prominent Nashvillians got too close to Tommy and "were forced to take to a friendly tree and only escaped after Tommy had decided he had kept them aloft long enough."

In the fall of 1904, both Gen. Jackson and his son William Harding were dead, Belle Meade's long career as a breeding establishment was over, and the farm was for sale. In November, "a splendid array of household furniture, historical relics and one of the best racehorse libraries in the country were sold." With the earlier sale of the horses, only Gen. Harding's household goods and a herd of 250 deer and seven elk remained. Nashvillians were interested in their fate.

Moses H. Cone, a North Carolina cotton merchant, purchased twenty of the deer to put on his estate at Blowing Rock. However, when an attempt was made to capture a dozen of the deer by driving them into a corral, "the frenzied animals dashed themselves against the sides of the enclosure and were either killed or severely maimed." One big buck sprang into the air and cleared the 12-foot-high fence "as though it was a small log." James B. Richardson, the administrator of his son-in-law William Harding Jackson's estate, called off the sale, not wanting to see the animals slaughtered.

In May 1906, when construction began on roads through the deer park, the dynamite frightened the deer. Consequently, the State of Tennessee bought the entire herd for $600 and turned them loose. Col. Joseph H. Acklen, state game warden, bought one elk and took it to his mansion, "Acklen," as a pet. Later, dogs severely injured it, making it necessary to have one of the elk's legs amputated. Finding it impossible to keep the elk at his home, Acklen gave the elk to the inmates at the Tennessee State Prison. They fashioned an artificial leg for it.

In 1906, Nashville's first unofficial zoo closed. Fortunately, there was a real zoo a few miles away called Glendale that opened in 1888. Still, Nashvillians would miss the Belle Meade deer park. It is likely the deer, so prevalent in the City of Belle Meade today, are descendants of the deer once in the Belle Meade deer park.

Nashville Once Boasted a Zoo Near Oak Hill

The Contributor 3/30/2015

In the 1880s, Nashville entrepreneur James E. Caldwell assembled, either through purchase or use of his own land, some sixty-eight acres five miles out of the city near the intersection of today's Lealand and Glendale Lanes for a public park. Later known as Glendale Park and Zoo—but first known as Woodstock—it quickly became intertwined with Nashville's social life and remained so for almost half a century.

Concurrently, Caldwell organized and built a street car line to the park. When the line opened with engines running at twenty miles an hour, and with open cars for summer travel and closed cars for winter, people packed the cars like sardines. Boys often rode on top of the cars. Caldwell sold the car line in 1889.

Glendale Park and Zoo   Collection of Ridley Wills II

In 1903, the several street railway lines in Nashville were merged into one entity, the Nashville Railway and Light Company, which then owned Glendale Park. To make the park more attractive, Percy Warner, company president, enlarged the zoo.

In 1925, the Dixie Highway opened over Monteagle Mountain, enabling Midwesterners to travel by automobile through Nashville and Chattanooga to Florida. Although fewer people rode streetcars as the popularity of automobiles increased, the park and zoo still made money and the officers of Nashville Railway and Light Company hoped to continue them. Unfortunately, inadequate parking and automobile competition proved to be overwhelming. The utility company closed Glendale Park and Zoo in 1932.

People

Roy Acuff

The Contributor 5/9/2016

In 1942, Roy Acuff and songwriter Fred Rose started Acuff-Rose Music. With Rose's ASCAP connections and Acuff's ability as a talent scout, Acuff-Rose became the most important publishing company in the industry. In 1946, the company signed Hank Williams and in 1950 published their first major hit, Patti Page's rendition of "Tennessee Waltz."

A detour in Acuff's music career came in 1948, when he ran for governor as the Republican nominee. With no political experience.

Roy lost badly to Gordon Browning. Having left the Opry, Acuff spent several years touring the Western United States. Demand for his appearances gradually dropped as the public turned to younger stars such as Ernest Tubb and Eddie Arnold. Nevertheless, in 1962, Acuff became the first living inductee in the Country Music Hall of Fame.

The 1970s saw an Acuff comeback with such popular albums as *Night*

Country music legend Roy Acuff
Acuff Rose Artists Corp.

Train to Memphis (1970), *I Saw the Light* (1971), *Will the Circle Be Unbroken* (1972), and *Wabash Cannonball* (1975).

A highlight of Roy Acuff's career came on March 16, 1974, when the Grand Ole Opry moved from Ryman Auditorium to the Grand Ole Opry House at Opryland. That night, President Richard Nixon was on stage with Roy, who gave him a quick lesson on how to spin a yo-yo. After his wife died, Roy moved to a small house at Opryland in the early '80s and continued to perform daily on stage.

In 1991, Acuff was given a lifetime achievement award by the John F. Kennedy Center for the Performing Arts, the first time the award was given to a country music performer. That same year, he was awarded the National Medal of Art. Roy Acuff died in Nashville on November 23, 1992, at age eighty-nine.

Ben Allen: Nashville's Mystic

The Contributor 5/26/2021

In the early 1900s, Nashville children would have been terrified at the thought of walking or running by the tall brick home of the city's mystic, the elegant Ben Allen, at 125 Eighth Avenue South (Rosa Parks Boulevard). Born in New Orleans in 1855, Ben moved to Nashville with his parents as a small child. His father, Joseph W. Allen, had made a fortune as a cotton broker in New Orleans and, in Nashville, helped found Third National Bank that later merged with First American National Bank. He also helped organize the Nashville Gas Company.

Allen and his wife built their imposing town house with tall arched windows in 1869 on what was then one of the fashionable residential streets, the part of Spruce Street that lay just south of Broadway. Mrs. Allen was such a perfectionist that she would not allow coal to be brought in the house until the coal had been washed.

Ben, although studious, dropped out of college to pursue his own studies. In 1883, he married a young widow, Susan Dorothy Perkins, eight years his senior. Later, Ben's parents turned over their big house to him and "Miss Sue" and moved to a smaller house. Ben and Sue moved in and Ben built a workshop in the back of his house where he designed jewelry and engraved silver. Ben also joined Nashville's Scottish Rite, a fraternal organization, while his gregarious wife entertained friends at small dinner parties.

Allen became a Mason in 1888 when he was thirty-three. He later rose to the lofty rank of 33rd degree Mason. Ben was considered a genius by those who knew him. Starting in boyhood, he delved into scholarly books on philosophy, astronomy, astrology, oriental history, and the history of art. He became a collector of paintings, statues, and oriental rugs.

Tall and slender with piercing blue eyes and a carefully groomed beard, Allen was always elegantly dressed, often in white linen. Stories of his mystic powers grew as more and more people attended his seances, which he held three times a week. There, the participants, usually friends or neighbors, sat around a table, touched fingers and waited for messages to come from the spirit world. Strangely, it was "Miss Sue" who received the messages. "The thing" came rushing in, rustling the ladies' voluminous petticoats. Some participants said "the thing" felt like a large cat rubbing against their legs. Others said "It unbuttoned high topshoes, rattled silver and china, and even caused the table to rise and push aside the people around it."

When Robert Love Taylor was governor between 1897 and 1899, he and his wife lived in the Maxwell House. Their grandson, Peter Taylor, the author, told the story of the morning when his grand-

mother Taylor suffered from a terrible headache. She tried to wait it out by sitting on the balcony overlooking the lobby. Without her knowledge, Allen hypnotized her and cured her of the headache. She was grateful and

Maxwell House

told the governor what happened. He replied, "I don't want you to be hypnotized again."

Once a skeptic at one of Allen's seances turned on the lights to expose what he considered a hoax. He was followed home that summer night by "the thing" that pulled off his bed covers several nights in a row.

When Ben Allen, Nashville's well-bred gentleman of leisure, grew seriously ill at age fifty-three, some Nashvillians thought that he had "brain fever." When he died in 1910, at fifty-five, his funeral was held at McKendree Methodist Church. At the stroke of midnight on Thursday, July 14, the eerie ceremony began. The Preceptor, Joseph Toy Howell, the only one wearing a white robe, took his place at the head of the casket. Four Knights with swords guarded the casket. Allen's own sword, shining with diamonds, rubies, amethysts, and other precious stones, lay on top of the casket. In the darkened church, Howell asked the Knights several questions, which they answered while kneeling beside the casket. The Preceptor then slowly struck an iron cross three times. The black-robed Knights then removed Allen's jeweled sword and other symbols of the riches of the world and solemnly left the church in a procession. The service took an hour. Today, people who travel Ben Allen Road in East Nashville have no idea who Ben Allen was.

Mills Darden: Tennessee's Largest Man

The Contributor 3/16/2022

Mills Darden, who was born near Rich Square, North Carolina, on October 7, 1799, is alleged to have been one of the largest men in history. He was reported to have stood about 7 feet 6 inches tall and was said to have weighed between 1,000 and 1,100

pounds. He settled in Henderson County, Tennessee, in about 1830 where he was an innkeeper and farmer. His second wife, Mary, who died in 1837 at age forty, stood only 4 feet 11 inches tall and weighed 98 pounds. The tallest of his seven children reached a height of 5'11".

Despite his gargantuan size, Darden was fairly active. He was known to be able to toss 500-pound bales of hay and carry twelve seed sacks weighing 1,200 pounds for over a mile. Some men in Henderson County once measured his weight by marking the exact point his one-horse cart, which had springs, lowered to when he sat in it. Later, when Mills was not there, they placed large rocks on the cart to see just how much weight it would take to match Mills sitting on it. They concluded that he weighed over 1,000 pounds.

Mills died in 1857 at the age of fifty-six. His physician reported that he died of strangulation due to rolls of fat around his windpipe. Some accounts say that it took seventeen men to put Darden in his coffin and that an entire wall had to be removed to get the coffin out. He was buried near his home on Mills Darden Cemetery Road five miles southwest of Lexington, Tennessee.

Civil Rights Icons Julian Bond and John Lewis Had Nashville Ties

The Contributor 2/13/2019

Civil Rights activist Julian Bond was born January 14, 1940, in Hubbard Hospital in Nashville, where his grandfather taught at Pearl High School. A great-grandfather, Aaron Brown, was, I believe, the son of a White businessman named Louis Lishey, who had a floral business on Lishey Avenue in East Nashville. Aaron Brown lived with the Lisheys, who gave him a greenhouse to start his own nursery business. After his death, Brown, who was considered Black, was buried near the Lisheys in Spring Hill Cemetery.

After Julian Bond's father, Horace Mann Bond, was named president of Lincoln University in Oxford, Pennsylvania, the Bond family moved there. In Oxford, Julian attended a public school, where he was named the brightest boy in the sixth grade. He then went to the George School outside Philadelphia. When Horace Bond was named president of Atlanta University, his family relocated to Atlanta where Julian attended and graduated from Morehouse College.

From 1960 to 1966, Bond organized and became the communications director of the Student Nonviolent Coordinating Committee (SNCC). In that role, he got to know John Lewis, an African American his age, who was also a cofounder of SNCC and a veteran of the Freedom Ride to Alabama and Mississippi where he was injured and jailed. Bond could relate to that as he, between 1960 and 1963, led student protests against segregation in public facilities in Georgia.

From 1966 to 1975, Julian Bond served in the Georgia House of Representatives. In 1976, he won a seat in the Georgia Senate. He gave this up to run for Congress where his friend from SNCC days, Lewis, defeated him. Bond and Morris Dees founded the Southern Poverty Law Center in Montgomery, Alabama. Bond was its president from 1971 until 1979. The Southern Poverty Law Center fights hate groups in America.

During the early 1990s, Julian Bond was visiting professor at Harvard and UVA. From 1998 to 2002 or later, he was chairman of the NAACP.

In about 2014, having discovered that Julian Bond was born in Nashville, where his family had lived for at least four generations, I contacted him by e-mail at the University of Virginia, where he was teaching. When I told him something about his Nashville ties, he quickly responded: "Ridley, you know more about my Nashville ties than I do. Keep me informed if you find out more."

John Lewis, a native of Troy, Alabama, in the "Black Belt," had seen, when he was six years old, only two White people in his life. A graduate of both American Baptist Theological Seminary and Fisk University, both in Nashville, Lewis was a leader in the Nashville sit-ins of 1960. In 1963, he was one of the "Big Six" leaders who organized

the 1963 march on Wash-
ington. Lewis went on to be
one of the great Civil Rights
leaders of the late twentieth
and early twenty-first centuries. In 2011, he received
the Presidential Medal of
Freedom Award. Today, he
is serving his 17th term in
the U.S. House of Repre-
sentatives from Georgia.

John Lewis and Nashville police officers, 1963
Nashville Public Library Special Collections

John Lewis frequently
returns to Nashville where
he proudly says he got his
start in civil rights work. He also is proud of having been educated at
American Baptist Theological Seminary and Fisk University.

[Editor's note: After John Lewis died July 17, 2020, Nashville
renamed Fifth Avenue North the "John Lewis Way" in recognition of
his remarkable life.]

Julian Bond, left, and John Lewis were part of the "Heroes of the Civil Rights
Movement" panel at the 2014 Civil Rights Summit, hosted by the LBJ Presidential
Library in Austin, Texas.   Photo by Lauren Gerson

Horticulture, Mental Health, and a Confederate Spy

(Dr. and Mrs. William Archer Cheatham)

The Contributor 6/20/2016

In 1847, the well-known philanthropist, Miss Dorothy L. Dix, visited Nashville, where she found the accommodations for the mentally insane woefully inadequate. She spoke to the State Legislature and influenced that body to pass an act on February 5, 1848, establishing a "hospital for the insane" about six miles from the city on the Murfreesboro Turnpike.

On the recommendation of prominent Nashville physician Dr. W. K. Bowling, Dr. William Archer Cheatham, who practiced medicine with Dr. Bowling, was named superintendent of the new facility. Cheatham thus became one of the elite group of mental health professionals, the asylum superintendents, "whose medical education and public and professional standing were considered superior to other medical practitioners."

In 1852, Cheatham officially left his private practice and devoted most of his time to the study of insanity, becoming Tennessee's first mental health professional and, in effect, the state's first psychiatrist. He supervised construction of the new four-story building designed by architect Adolphus Heiman, who also designed at least part of Belle Monte for Adelicia and Joseph A. S. Acklen. Cheatham later supervised the construction of two hospital wings, enabling the hospital to accommodate 250 patients as originally planned. Dr. Cheatham and his wife, the former Mary Ready, of Murfreesboro, moved to a home built on the grounds of the asylum in 1852. Their children, Martha Strong and Richard B., were born there in 1853 and 1855 respectively. Dr. Cheatham was interested in horticulture, particularly as it related to mental health. He added a horticulturalist to the hospital staff and built a greenhouse on the hospital grounds for native and exotic flowers and shrubs. As part of their therapy, patients who were able and willing, participated in gardening and raising crops on the large farm that was part of the property. In about 1861, Dr. Cheatham's contract was renewed for another eight years, and he was beginning to receive national recognition when the Union army captured Nashville in February 1862.

Andrew Johnson, a political opponent of Dr. Cheatham's cousin, Robert B. Cheatham, who was Nashville's mayor, wasted no time when he was appointed military governor of Tennessee, in replacing Dr. Cheatham as superintendent of the asylum and R. B. Cheatham as mayor. Later, Mary Cheatham was accused of being a spy after exchanging letters with her sister, Mattie, who was married to Confederate Gen. John Hunt Morgan.

The Cheathams were arrested and sent to Louisville en route to prison in Alton, Illinois. After Mary became too ill to travel any farther, Dr. and Mrs. Cheatham were placed under house arrest in a Louisville hotel. Finally, they were allowed to return home after agreeing to take the oath of allegiance and give bond.

Mary died April 27, 1864. In the winter of 1866–67, Dr. Cheatham began dating Adelicia Acklen, the widow of Joseph Acklen. By spring, everyone knew that they planned to marry, realizing that they shared interests in horticulture, greenhouses, fine paintings, and sculpture. They married that year. In addition to his private practice in Nashville, Dr. Cheatham spent a considerable amount of time overseeing

Tennessee State Asylum for the Insane

Adelicia's plantations in Louisiana. In 1885, Adelicia was restless. She purchased lots in Orlando, Florida, where she intended to build a house. She quickly changed her mind and refocused on Washington, D.C., where she acquired a house on Iowa Circle in the much more sophisticated Washington, D.C. She would never return to Nashville. In 1887, Adelicia sold her Belmont mansion and began building a house at 1776 Massachusetts Ave. in Washington. Dr. Cheatham, having no interest in leaving Nashville, moved to the Maxwell House. He always felt his crowning achievement was not his marriage to Adelicia but his contributions to mental health. He and Adolphus Heiman envisioned, planned, and supervised the construction of the Tennessee Hospital for the Insane. It grieved Dr. Cheatham that, in the post-war period, the state did not have the financial resources to continue operating the hospital on the scale he had established.

Dr. Cheatham was a great-great-grandfather of my wife, Irene Jackson Wills.

Marvin T. Duncan

The Contributor 7/6/2015

Marvin T. Duncan, the founder of Duncan School, got his education at Webb School and at Vanderbilt, where he graduated in 1905. After teaching at Wallace School and at Massey School, he started Duncan School in September 1908. His wife, Pauline, served as assistant principal. She also was chair of the mathematics department. Mr. Duncan, who strongly believed in emphasizing the classics, taught Latin. The school was located on 25th Avenue South adjacent to the current site of Vanderbilt's Memorial Gymnasium, and a large number of its graduates attended Vanderbilt.

Mr. Duncan said that "the chief purpose of the school is to prepare boys for the best colleges and universities, and at the same time to give them a practical education. We hope to instill within them a love for truth and scholarship and an appreciation for the higher things in life.

The true object of an education is to develop the character and train the mind of one in such a way that he may be able to assume leadership." Because of declining health, Mr. Duncan closed his school at the end of the 1951–1952 school year.

Whitten Duncan Home, 4414 Granny White Pike
Courtesy of Carney (Mrs. Alfred) Farris

Carl and Otto Giers

The Contributor 10/13/2021

Carl Giers was a German-American who had a photograph studio in Nashville. He was born April 28, 1828, in Bonn, Germany, came to the United States in 1845, and made Nashville his home in 1852. Three years later, Carl began his career as a photographer. During the Civil War, he photographed soldiers around Nashville—first Confederate and, after February 1862, when Nashville fell to the Union army, Union soldiers.

In 1870, Carl and his wife, Pauline, adopted two children of deceased friends, Peter and Barbara Burkhardt—Otto Burkhardt, then twelve, and his little sister, Katie, then six. In 1876, Carl put together Tennessee's exhibition at the United States Centennial Exposition in Philadelphia.

When Otto was older, he and Carl were both members of the Knights Templar. Otto was nineteen when Carl died.

In 1883, at age twenty-five, Otto decided to try his hand as a photographer. He and some other German-American friends living in Nashville formed Thuss, Koellein, & Giers, Photographers, and late the next year Otto began a remarkable series of documentary photographs of Nashville's streets, schools, churches, homes, and government buildings.

Otto Giers
Nashville: The Faces of Two Centuries

1999 and 2000, Jim Hoobler published two volumes of paperbacks entitled *Nashville from the Collection of Carl and Otto Giers*, which are available today at Randy Elder's Bookstore at 101 White Bridge Road.

Otto Giers lived at 1619 Eighteenth Avenue South, next door to Nashville author and educator, Alfred Leland Crabb, who served as one of his pallbearers. Today, my wife, Irene, and I live in a penthouse condominium earlier owned by Sarah Hunter Hicks Green Marks, Otto's granddaughter, who made available to Hoobler the photographs in his two-volume paperback.

The Remarkable Adventures of Richard Halliburton (1900–1939)

The Contributor 12/26/2019

My grandfather, Ridley Wills, was born in Brownsville, Tennessee, September 19, 1871. When his father, Dr. Thaddeus Wills, died of a heart attack in 1878 while making his rounds on horseback treating people for yellow fever, Dr. Wills's widow was left to rear her two boys, Mann and Ridley, alone. As so many enterprising young people in small towns do, Ridley left Brownsville as a young man to seek fame and fortune in Nashville. He accomplished this by co-founding in 1901, with C. "Neely" Craig, the National Life and Accident Insurance Company. In time Ridley became nationally known as an expert on weekly premium life insurance.

Ridley had an aunt in Brownsville, Eva Mann Moore, who was very proud of Ridley and of another young man on the other side of her family. His name was Richard Halliburton. He too was born in Brownsville, on January 9, 1900, a generation younger than Ridley. Richard moved to Memphis, where he grew up. His favorite course as a schoolboy was geography. He attended Memphis University School and Hutchison School before going off to Lawrenceville Prep School in New Jersey. There, he was chief editor of the *Lawrence*.

Halliburton next attended Princeton University where he was on the editorial board of and edited the *Princetonian Pictorial Magazine*. In 1919, Halliburton dropped out of school to walk around England and France before returning to Princeton, to get his degree. His travels in Europe solidified his desire to live an unconventional life, and to make a living by writing about his adventures. Although he did not have an athletic build, one of his early escapades was to swim the length of the Panama Canal. Only ships were allowed to navigate the canal, so Halliburton registered himself as the *SS Halliburton*, paid the lowest fee in history, 36 cents, based on his length and weight, and swam the canal, Atlantic to Pacific.

In 1925, Bobbs-Merrill published Halliburton's first book, which became the first of many best-sellers for him. Halliburton was also one of the most successful lecturers in the years between the two World Wars. His vivid reenactments of his adventures helped to popularize adventure journalism.

Halliburton never married. In his youth, he courted girls and was infatuated with at least two. As he matured, he became bisexual but kept his sexual orientation a secret from the public and his parents, who wanted grandchildren. He was a friend and may have been a lover of one of the first openly gay film stars of the day, Ramon Novarro.

Halliburton commissioned William Alexander Levy, a twenty-seven-year-old architect, to build a modern house. Levy was the lover of Paul Mooney, Halliburton's editor and ghostwriter. The concrete box house was suspended between canyon and ocean in Laguna Beach, California. The three men, Levy, Halliburton, and Mooney, each had separate bedrooms. People in Laguna Beach soon dubbed it "Hangover House."

In 1930, Halliburton hired Moye Stephens on a handshake, but no salary, to fly him around the world in an open cockpit biplane, a modified Stearman CV-3B named *The Flying Carpet*. Halliburton promised to pay Stephens's expenses. It was an epic journey that took 18 months to cover 33,000 miles and visit 34 countries. The two men took off on Christmas Day 1930 from Los Angeles and flew to New York. There they crated the plane and shipped it to London while they took a ship to London, where the extended flight began. They first flew to France, then to Spain, Gibraltar and Fez, Morocco, where Stephens performed aerobatics. Next, they flew over the Atlas Mountains and crossed the Sahara to Timbuktu.

Their next stop was in Algeria where they spent several weeks with the French Foreign Legion before continuing on to Cairo and Damascus. In Persia (Iran), they met the celebrated German aviatrix, Elly Beinhorn, whose plane had been forced down due to mechanical failure. They assisted her before meeting Crown Princess Mahin Banu, whom Stephens gave a ride in the open cockpit. In neighboring Iraq, Stephens gave young Crown Prince Ghazi a ride over his school yard. At their next stop in India, Halliburton visited the Taj Mahal. They then flew to Mt. Everest, where Richard made the first aerial photograph of the famous mountain. In Nepal, Stephens performed aerobatics for the Maharajah of Nepal. In Borneo, they were fed by Sylvia Brett, the wife of the white Rajah of Sarawak. Stephens gave her a brief ride, making her the first woman in that country to fly. At the Rajang River, Stephens took the chief of the Dayak headhunters for a flight. In gratitude, the chief gave them 60 kilos of shrunken heads, which they dumped as soon as possible. They were the first

Americans to fly to the Philippines. In Manila, they crated the plane and shipped it to San Francisco. They took a ship to San Francisco, where they uncrated the plane and flew to Los Angeles. This was the final leg of their trip, which cost Halliburton $50,000 plus fuel. His book about the flight earned Halliburton royalties of $100,000 in its first year.

On March 3, 1939, Halliburton began a new extremely dangerous venture. He decided to sail on the junk named *Sea Dragon* from Hong Kong across the Pacific, intending to land in San Francisco where he wanted to visit the Golden Gate International Exposition. His crew were skipper John Welsh; engineer Henry Von Fehren; and crew members John Potter and Gordon Torrey, both recent Dartmouth graduates.

The *Sea Dragon* venture was jinxed from the start. The construction of the Chinese junk was plagued by cost overruns and engineering problems. Its crew managed to sail the boat halfway across the Pacific when an unexpected typhoon struck on March 24, 1939. The junk was last sighted by the liner *SS President Coolidge*, which was having

Richard Halliburton and the *Sea Dragon*
South China Morning Post, March 22, 2014

trouble itself dealing with huge waves, some 1900 km west of Midway Island. In the midst of the storm, the *SS President Coolidge* received a cheerful radio message from the junk skipper that said, "Having a wonderful time. Wish you were here instead of me." A second message was more somber. After giving their location, speed and course, Welsh said, "Heavy rain squalls, high seas, when closer may we avail ourselves of your direction finder? Regards, Welsh." That was the last message anyone ever heard from the *Sea Dragon*.

After a US Navy search by ships and planes for the missing junk that covered thousands of square miles, the rescue attempt was called off. In 1945, some wreckage was found washed ashore on the California coastline that was identified as a rudder believed to belong to the *Sea Dragon*.

Richard Halliburton was officially declared dead by the Memphis Chancery Court on October 5, 1939. He was thirty-nine years old.

Susan L. Heron and Ida E. Hood

The Contributor 1/6/2021

Susan L. Heron and Ida E. Hood, neither of whom are well known in Nashville, were the founders of Belmont College for Young Women, located at Belmont, earlier the estate of Adelicia Acklen Cheatham. Little is known of their lives before they moved south to become co-principals of Martin College in Pulaski, Tennessee. Hood may have been from Philadelphia and Heron from Iowa. They met as classmates in Philadelphia and became great friends, announcing themselves to everyone as "Hood and Heron."

After five years at Martin College, they moved to Nashville in 1890 and founded Belmont College. Despite being Northerners, they educated young women in an atmosphere of Southern manners. Their classes included academic achievement in the subjects of Latin, Greek, and mathematics, all required courses, as well as more conventional courses for young ladies—elocution, gymnastics, and music. The two

founders were devoted to their students and to the school, construct-
ing new buildings, a swimming pool and riding stables.

Heron was strong-willed, and red-headed, the embodiment of gra-
ciousness and dignity. Hood was gentle, loved poetry, and encouraged
the students to achieve what was expected of them.

Hood and Heron retired in 1913, selling Belmont to its rival
school, Ward Seminary. The ladies built "Braeburn," a beautiful home
at 211 Deer Park Drive in 1916 and retired there. Susan Heron
died in 1921 while Ida Hood lived until 1933. Their graves are side
by side in Mt. Olivet Cemetery
where they share a single monument whose inscription is titled
"Hood-Heron." Braeburn is now
owned by Vanderbilt University.
[Editor's note: Braeburn was sold
by Vanderbilt in 2021.]

Founders of Belmont College
for Young Women, Ida Hood
and Susan Heron, on the
mansion's steps
Belmont University website

Mary Randolph Custis and Robert E. Lee

The Contributor early 2022

After watching on television a crane remove the statue of Robert
E. Lee from its position on Monument Boulevard in Richmond,
I decided to read John Perry's book, *Lady of Arlington: The Life of
Mrs. Robert E. Lee,* to learn more about Lee's family and their status
as slaveowners. I learned a great deal by doing so.

Robert E. Lee's wife, Mary Anna Randolph Custis Lee, inherited her father's home, "Arlington," when he died in 1857. In his will,

George Washington Custis left his home and its contents, 1,100 surrounding acres, sixty-three slaves, a mill, and other lands in Alexandria and Fairfax Counties, Virginia to Mary. He also inserted a provision in his will that, five years after his death, the slaves he left Mary should be emancipated. So, on December 5, 1862, following Lee's great victory over the Union Army at Fredericksburg, Robert E. Lee left his army in charge of Generals Stonewall Jackson and James Longstreet and went to the courthouse in Spotsylvania County, Virginia where he filed a deed of manumission freeing his wife's slaves and all other Custis plantation slaves in accordance with the terms in his father-in-law's will. This meant that, when Lincoln issued, on New Year's Day, 1863, his emancipation proclamation, freeing slaves in states still in rebellion, the Arlington slaves were already free. Lee said at the time of their manumission, "They are entitled to their freedom and I wish to give it to them." From then on, neither Robert E. Lee nor Mary had any slaves. Neither believed in slavery but both felt that, without education or property, freed slaves would never be able to make their own way. Mary was in favor of freeing slaves and sending them to Liberia. Lee was not, feeling that they would be worse off there than in America.

Throughout the war, most of which time she was living in Richmond, Mary still harbored the conviction that her plantation, Arlington, across the Potomac from Washington, had been illegally seized by the Federal Government in the spring of 1861 and that someday it should be rightfully returned to her.

Edwin M. Stanton, Lincoln's Secretary of War, had other ideas. He wanted to make it as difficult and expensive as possible to restore the property to the Lees once the war was over. So he ordered the U.S. Army to seize the property. The army did. Farm fences were taken down and crops destroyed. The army built an enormous stable complex to house horses and mules that served the military units in and around Washington. New fences and outbuildings went up on the grounds.

The winter of 1861–62 was unseasonably wet and the immaculate Arlington grounds were soon churned into "a thick froth of knee-deep muck that never dried." Higher up on Arlington Heights, "a large rambling convalescent hospital" was built for wounded and sick Union soldiers. Down by the river, around the famous Arlington Spring and the old Custis picnic grounds, hordes of penniless, Black people built shanties, and each day searched for food and work. In time, a Freedman's Village was erected there, with government-built roads, workshops, a hospital, a home for the aged, and other buildings for a population of African Americans that exceeded 2,000.

To further humiliate Robert E. Lee and his wife, Stanton ordered his Quartermaster General Montgomery C. Meigs to turn "one of the most storied estates in the country into a graveyard." Meigs approached his job with relish as he considered Lee to be the vilest traitor of all. Meigs ordered the first graves to be dug encircling the great white mansion as close to it as possible. He was furious when the first burials, on May 13, 1864, were made a half-mile away near the old slave graveyard. Meigs ordered that they be moved closer to the mansion.

On June 15, 1864, Meigs wrote a letter suggesting that the land immediately surrounding Arlington be named a national cemetery. He personally went to the grounds with a surveyor where they marked off plots for a long row of graves along the border of Mary's flower garden. Later in May, Secretary of War Stanton issued an order designating Arlington as a National Cemetery.

In May 1873, an arthritic crippled Mary Custis Lee rode out in a carriage to see her old home for the first time since 1861. As the carriage turned up the carriageway to the house, Mrs. Lee saw the stumps of

Civil War federal soldiers in front of Arlington, the home of Gen. Robert E. Lee and his wife, Mary   National Archives

magnificent trees that once adorned the grounds. Now, headstones of soldiers seemed to be everywhere. Down toward Arlington Spring, she saw the humble buildings of the Freedman's village that stretched for block after block. At the crest of the hill, she saw a semblance of her old flower garden still there, maintained by a faithful emancipated slave named Ephraim. Over the front doorway of Arlington mansion, she read a sign that said "Cemetery Office." Mary, sickened by what she saw, never got out of the carriage.

When Mary Custis Lee died in the fall of 1873, her oldest son, Custis Lee, who was supposed to inherit Arlington, took up her fight for the return of the home to him. In 1882, the case came before the United States Supreme Court which ruled that Arlington had been improperly confiscated and ordered that it be returned to its rightful owner, Custis Lee. So, nine years after her painful final visit to Arlington, Mary Custis Lee was posthumously vindicated. Her son, Custis had no interest in living in the middle of a cemetery and, immediately after acquiring its ownership, sold the estate to the U.S. Government for $150,000.

Custis was president of Washington & Lee College at the time of the sale, a position he assumed following his father's death in 1870. He would remain president until his retirement in 1897 when he took up residence at "Ravensworth" an ancestral Virginia home, where he died in 1913. Custis Lee, while overshadowed by his famous father, had been first in his 1854 graduating class at West Point. He later served as a brigadier general in the Confederate Army. His younger brother, William Henry Fitzhugh "Rooney" Lee, who was educated at Harvard, also fought in the Civil War. Badly wounded at Gettysburg, he was captured by the Union army. Nine months later, he was exchanged and, on February 18, 1865, was appointed brigadier general by President Davis. For unknown reasons, Rooney declined the appointment. After the war he lived with his wife's sister and her husband in the Valley of the Yadkin (Wilkes County, North Carolina) where he died in 1889.

The Kingfish Comes to Nashville

The Contributor 3/4/2020

In 1934, United States senator and former governor of Louisiana Huey "Kingfish" Long decided to take all 1,500 cadets at Louisiana State University to Nashville for the football game on October 27 between the LSU Tigers and the Vanderbilt Commodores. He said his interest in doing so was his admiration for Vanderbilt's heralded coach, Dan McGugin, who would retire at the end of the 1934 season. Long said that McGugin and Russ Cohen, an assistant coach at Vanderbilt, helped LSU out when the state university was about to get kicked out of the Southern Conference, and "I'm gonna help them as much as I can," the Kingfish said. Long also knew that the trip would advertise LSU and Huey Long. He called the traffic manager of the Illinois Central Railroad, which controlled the greater part of the route to Nashville. He told the agent he was taking several thousand LSU students to Nashville for a football game and wanted a reasonable round-trip rate. The man replied that the rates were set and the fare would have to be $19 a person. The Kingfish said, "That's too much. I'll give you $6 per person." Scorning to deal further with underlings, Long called the railroad president in Chicago and told him he wanted a cheap rate to Nashville and back. Long casually mentioned that the Illinois Central Railroad owned bridges in Louisiana that were worth much more than they were assessed. It was quite possible, he said, that the Louisiana Tax Commission would decide to assess these properties at their true value.

The next day, the railroad president called Long and told him he could have the $6 rate. The railroad's senior management team had no doubt that Huey would follow through on his threat if they failed to comply. Privately, they were furious, but realized that it would be smart to please the powerful Long. Huey was euphoric. He called James Monroe Smith, the president of LSU, and told him to cancel classes on October 27.

The LSU contingent would travel to Nashville in six separate trains, each with fourteen cars, and each painted a different eye-catching color. On the sides of the cars were signs proclaiming "Hurrah for Huey."

One of the Kingfish's prides were the 1,500 LSU cadets. He invited all of them to, for $6, ride in the "red" train, one of six trains he commandeered to take an estimated 5,000 LSU fans and students to the game. To ensure that the cadet corp would look good in Nashville, Senator Long bought each one of them a new, gray uniform. For those who could not afford to pay the $6 fare, he loaned them the money.

In the second car, called the white train, the Kingfish rode with his wife, a son, and a few friends. Each of the six trains had a kitchen car that served sandwiches and coffee. The Kingfish allowed no drinking on the trip. To enforce this and to provide order on the trains, where the boys sat up all night, and in Nashville, Huey took along twenty-five armed Louisiana State policemen who walked through each car throughout the trip to make sure nobody went wild. Having state police caused a problem because they were not legally able to act as policemen in Tennessee. To solve this, the Tennessee Game and Fish Commission deputized them as game wardens as soon as they arrived in Nashville.

Just before boarding the white train, Huey was asked if he would use the occasion to announce his candidacy for president of the United States in 1936 on his "share-the-wealth" platform. His response was

Huey "Kingfish" Long had a train like this transport Louisiana State University cadets to the October 27, 1934, football game between the Tigers and Vanderbilt's Commodores.

Huey Long, A Biography, Office of Information Services, LSU

that, if he ran for president, it would probably be for president of Mexico. He also turned down an invitation to speak on behalf of Tennessee Democratic candidates. He said he did not have time, but said he planned to speak at the game, although he refused to say what his subject would be.

Before leaving Baton Rouge, Long dispatched sound trucks to Nashville as an advance guard. Obviously, he was going to speak somewhere.

A third car carried the 125-piece Louisiana State Band. Because none of the members had a banjo, the Kingfish ordered the train master to telegraph the mayor of Vicksburg to put a banjo aboard when the band train reached that city. As an afterthought, Huey told the station master, "I would sort of like a pair of fiddlers too." Huey then sent for a singer, already abroad. When the young man in a jersey appeared, the Kingfish said to him: "You say you sing for a living." Before the frightened boy could respond, Senator Long answered his own question, saying, "Well, it depends on how well you sing and how long you will live."

At 9 a.m. on Saturday October 27, Long led a parade in downtown Nashville, stopping at all the major hotels. Accompanying him were Nashville's mayor, Hilary E. Howe, and Vanderbilt coach Dan McGugin. Behind them came the 150-member LSU marching band.

Before the afternoon game in Dudley Field before 20,000 fans, the 1,500-member LSU cadet corps marched on the field in their handsome gray uniforms and, at halftime, Huey gave a brief talk, surrounded by his sound trucks. McGugin introduced him as, "the All-American football rooter of all time." In his talk, Long said that, except for LSU and Tulane, Vanderbilt was his favorite team. That afternoon, LSU administered Vanderbilt its worst defeat in fourteen years, winning 29–0. Outclassed, the Commodores never passed the LSU 22-yard line, completed only four of eighteen passes, and gained only 25 yards rushing. LSU's running backs, Mickal and Fatherree, couldn't be stopped. At the game, Huey was full of himself.

Long never ran for president although President Roosevelt worried that he would. Roosevelt felt that Long, whom he despised, was the most dangerous man in America.

In September 1935 in the State Capitol building in Baton Rouge, Huey was confronted by a man who came out from behind a pillar in the corridor. He brushed by security guards, and, when within a few feet of Senator Long, pulled out a small pistol and shot the Kingfish. The murderer, Carl Adam Weiss, was immediately gunned down by Long's security guards, who pumped thirty bullets in his lifeless body. Thirty hours after he was shot and slightly more than a week after he passed his 42nd birthday, Huey Long died on Monday afternoon, September 10, 1935. Most of those near his deathbed heard him say just before dying,

"God, don't let me die. I have so much to do."

The McNairys and the Lady from Boston

The Contributor 7/7/2021

In 1847, Dr. and Mrs. Boyd McNairy's mansion on Sumner Street had the reputation of being "Nashville's guest house." One guest that year was Miss Dorothy Lynde Dix of Boston, "America's most distinguished woman." Her visit in the closing months of 1847 was her third visit to Nashville. On all her visits she helped Dr. John Sims McNairy improve living conditions for inmates in the Tennessee Lunatic Asylum of which McNairy was superintendent. The asylum had opened in 1832.

Miss Dix realized in 1847 that many of the cells housing patients were underground and without proper ventilation. Those above ground were found by her to be inadequate because they were not heated properly. She told the Tennessee State Legislature the asylum was "wholly unfit for the habitation of human beings" and that they should appropriate the necessary funds to build a new hospital, which she said should have at least 200 acres of land and be accessible by good roads.

The House of Representative members enthusiastically thanked Miss Dix for her tireless work and approved the purchase of a large piece of land on the Murfreesboro Turnpike six miles southeast of

Nashville. They also approved the erection there of a new and costly hospital.

Unfortunately, Dr. McNairy did not live to see the hospital completed. He died at age thirty-five in August 1849, during a cholera epidemic. The day after his death, Gov. Neill S. Brown named John's father, Dr. Boyd McNairy, superintendent of the new hospital. Dr. and Mrs. McNairy moved to a home built for them on the asylum grounds, leaving their Sumner Street home vacant, until March 1, 1852, when Dr. McNairy, at age sixty-seven, passed asylum responsibility to a younger man, Dr. William Archer Cheatham. [See History Article #55 "Horticulture, Mental Health, and a Confederate Spy" for more information on Dr. Cheatham.] At that time, Dr. and Mrs. McNairy returned to their beloved Sumner Street home. Dr. McNairy, a distinguished citizen, a generous man, fine physician, and a skilled violinist, died November 21, 1856.

The Insane Asylum of Tennessee
Collection of Ridley Wills II

"Buddy" Morgan and Standing Up for Rev. James Lawson

The Contributor 8/14/2019

Born in Nashville in 1893, Hugh J. "Buddy" Morgan entered Vanderbilt University as an undergraduate in 1910. There, the strapping 6'4" 215-pounder was twice an All Southern center on the football team.

After receiving an MD from Johns Hopkins Medical School in 1918, Dr. Morgan was commissioned a first lieutenant in the Medical Section, Officers Reserve Corps, and served as an assistant surgeon in France during World War I.

Following the war, he returned to Hopkins as a staff member before becoming resident physician at the Rockefeller Institute. Dr. Morgan returned to Vanderbilt in 1924 as an associate professor of medicine. He was promoted to professor of clinical medicine in 1928 and, in 1935, became the hospital's physician-in-chief as well as professor of medicine and chair of the Department of Medicine.

During World War II, Dr. Morgan commanded Vanderbilt's 300th General Hospital Unit, and served as chief medical consultant in the office of the attorney general. In December 1942, he was promoted to brigadier general and named chief of the Medical Consultants Division, Office of the Surgeon General. There, he was responsible for supervising all medical work (excluding surgery) of the entire United States Army. For his outstanding work during World War II, he received the Distinguished Service Medal.

Dr. Hugh Morgan
Department of Medicine, Vanderbilt staff photo in *Recollections*

Early in 1946, Dr. Morgan returned to Vanderbilt as Professor of Medicine and Physician in Chief. He was soon chosen president of the American College of Physicians. After his retirement in 1958, Dr. Morgan was elected to the Vanderbilt Board of Trust. In 1960, he was the only member of that board to vote not to expel James Lawson, an African American divinity student, for his role in the Nashville sit-ins (see photo at right).

Photo by Vic Cooley, *Nashville Banner* Archives

Following Dr. Morgan's death on Christmas Eve 1961, the Vanderbilt Board of Trust named a graduate dormitory Morgan Hall in his honor. In 1989, Vanderbilt established the Hugh J. Morgan Chair of Medicine honoring Dr. Morgan for his twenty-three years as chairman of the Department of Medicine and for the contributions and significance of his life. Dr. Sidney Burwell, chair of the department of medicine at Vanderbilt from 1928 until 1935, said of Hugh Morgan: "He was a charming man with firm convictions. He was courteous, gallant, and had a warm, tinkling humor. He was delicately sensitive to and careful of the smallest human weakness and respected the well-groomed opinions of others. . . . During the period of his tenure as chair of the Department of Medicine from 1935 until 1958, the impact of his influence on clinical medicine, medical education, and, above all, on people was tremendous, not only at Vanderbilt, but throughout the United States and around the world."

Jesse Maxwell Overton

The Contributor 10/19/2015

Jesse Maxwell Overton was born July 25, 1863, in Pulaski, Tennessee, the fifth of John and Harriet Maxwell Overton's six children. He spent his childhood at Travellers Rest south of Nashville on the Franklin Pike. His childhood was filled with stories of the Civil War and particularly of the Battle of Nashville that was fought, in part, on Overton property.

Jesse was an excellent student who graduated from Harvard College in the class of 1886. Until he married, he lived at home with his parents. Jesse married the former Sarah "Saidee" Cheney Williams of Nashville on November 10, 1891. He and Saidee had three children—two girls, Elizabeth and Harriet, and a son, John Williams Overton, who was killed in World War I.

In 1900, Jesse and Saidee built "Overton Hall," a modern home built on the old Overton Plantation on the east side of

Overton Hall, home of Jesse and Saidee Overton, was built in 1900, six miles from Nashville on an old plantation on the east side of Franklin Pike.   Collection of Ridley Wills II

Franklin Pike six miles from town. The Tudor-style home stood in the midst of a large park, thickly forested with giant hardwood trees.

The land on which Overton Hall stood was granted by the U.S. government for service performed by Jesse Maxwell, who was Jesse Maxwell Overton's great-grandfather. At Overton Hall, Jesse and Saidee exemplified traditional Southern hospitality.

Although his business interests prevented him from attending Harvard University reunions, Jesse enjoyed having his Harvard classmates visit Overton Hall. Jesse and Saidee hosted Harvard's President Eliot there elegantly. Nashvillians also enjoyed Overton Hall's hospitality. Those who were privileged to know and attend parties given by Jesse Maxwell Overton "were charmed by his innate courtesy and breeding and the forcefulness and kindliness of his character." Positive in his views, Jesse was sound in his convictions and was respected by his peers. Overton had a reputation of never performing an unkind act or being guilty of an unjust sentiment.

Jesse raised Berkshire hogs and Jersey cattle at Overton Hall. Both herds were considered among the finest in the state. Vice president of the American Forestry Association, he was also president of the Tennessee Forestry Association. Overton was additionally a director of Fourth National Bank and owned Overton & Bush, a coal and ice company in Nashville.

Jesse Maxwell Overton died December 16, 1922, as the result of a collision between his automobile and a trolley car. The *Nashville Banner* editorialized, "From everything he achieved, this community benefited. While he was a businessman, he enjoyed to the fullest social intercourse with his friends. He was always in good humor and his laughter was contagious. His optimism pervaded."

Soon after her husband's death, Saidee Overton sold Overton Hall to Mr. and Mrs. Herbert Farrell, who renamed the house "Crieve Hall." Mrs. Overton moved across Franklin Pike where she built a two-story, Georgian brick house which she named "Beauvoir." It was on the high hill where the Holy Trinity Greek Orthodox Church stands today at 4905 Franklin Pike. Mrs. Overton's final move, made in about 1943, was to the Wellington Arms Apartment on Harding Road. She died in 1963. Crieve Hall on today's Farrell Parkway later burned.

President Theodore Roosevelt Honors a Former President during a 1907 Visit to Nashville

The Contributor 6/27/2016

When President Theodore Roosevelt visited Nashville on October 22, 1907, it was not as a stranger. In 1888, he spent some time in Nashville researching for his book, *Winning of the West*. He made a number of friends here, including Gen. William Hicks Jackson.

An enormous crowd of 150,000 people welcomed President Roosevelt on his 1907 visit. Fifteen thousand welcomed the president at Union Station, including Governor Patterson, Mayor Brown and many leading citizens. It took forty policemen, six Secret Service men, and a number of deputy sheriffs to handle the crowd at Union Station. Waiting for him outside were fifteen carriages and twenty-four

Former President Theodore Roosevelt was driven through the Peabody Normal campus on his way to the Hermitage, October 22, 1907.
Collection of Ridley Wills II

automobiles that formed a parade to take him to the Ryman Auditorium. The crowd was so thick at the corner of Eighth and Broad that the boom of the cannons on Capitol Hill firing a twenty-one-gun salute could hardly be heard.

At the Ryman, 6,000 people were crammed in the building to hear and see the president. Although he was scheduled to speak for ten minutes, Roosevelt spoke for thirty-two minutes. During his talk, he gave one of the greatest tributes ever paid to Andrew Jackson.

Roosevelt left the Ryman in an automobile to travel to The Hermitage. To make it easier, eighteen sprinkling carts had worked late in the night on the Lebanon Pike to ensure that dust would not be a nuisance to the president on his ride out.

Roosevelt arrived at The Hermitage at 11:30 and was there for an hour. He was greeted in the front hall by members of the Ladies Hermitage Association. In the dining room, Mrs. John M. Gray poured coffee which was served Roosevelt by Mrs. Rachael Jackson Lawrence. No one knows if the coffee, which the president enjoyed, was Maxwell House Coffee or H. G. Hill's "Fit for a King Coffee." As neither was a national brand, Roosevelt had never heard of either. The dining room table was decorated with crimson roses. The luncheon was served using the Jacksons' silver service.

Roosevelt spent some time touring the house where he showed a special interest in Jackson's library. Next, he walked out in the garden to the Jacksons' tomb, and spoke for ten minutes in front of it. In the garden, he was introduced to the son of Jackson's old bodyguard, Uncle Alfred. Before leaving the Hermitage to board his special train, the President was presented with a number of mementos of his visit, including a bottle of twenty-year-old Tennessee whiskey.

The run back to the city took only thirty minutes. Once there, he went directly to Union Station, where his train was ready to take him to Cowan, Tennessee, where Roosevelt's small pullman car was unshackled and attached to a small engine that took him up the mountain to speak at the University of the South.

Roosevelt slept the night after leaving Nashville in his pullman car. While in Nashville, he did not visit the Maxwell House, much less spend the night there. He never said that the coffee he tasted at the Hermitage was "good to the last drop." That was fabricated by Joel Cheek, who borrowed the words from Asa Candler, who said his Coca-Cola was "good to the last drop" a number of years earlier.

Col. Alford M. Shook
Spent His Last Years in Nashville

The Contributor 7/21/2021

Some of you reading this article, have been to Tracy City, Tennessee, most likely to buy salt-rising bread or sweet rolls at the Dutch Maid Bakery. About three blocks from the bakery is the elegant home built by Col. A.M. Shook in the last decades of the nineteenth century. Who was A. M. Shook, you might ask? Alfred Montgomery Shook was, in 1880, the general manager of the Tennessee Coal, Iron and Railroad Company, headquartered in Tracy City, then the largest town between Murfreesboro and Chattanooga.

Born at his father's farm in Franklin County in 1845, Alfred was sent by his parents at age thirteen to live with an uncle in Winchester, where A. M. went to school. His uncle was postmaster and had a drug store there. A. M. clerked in both these establishments to pay for his room and board.

During the Civil War, Shook served in the Confederate Army of Tennessee. After the war, A. M., still a young man, moved to Tracy City where he became interested in the coal and coke industry. By the 1870s, he occupied a position of responsibility with the Tennessee Coal, Iron and Railroad Company. By 1880, he was general manager, a position he held for a number of years.

Col. Shook encouraged his company's coal miners to build their own homes in Tracy City rather than live in the company's rough mining camp. In 1888–1889, he gave $39,700 dollars to build an imposing red brick school, which served the children of Tracy City

Col. A. M. Shook home in Tracy City, Tennessee
Courtesy the Heritage Center, Tracy City

until May 1976, when it burned to the ground. A local historian said that Shook built the school to benefit the children of his employees and the other children in Tracy City. To finance the school, Tennessee Coal, Iron and Railroad Company, deducted 50 cents to a dollar from the paychecks of its employees to ensure that the school had the funds needed to operate for nine months every year. The paycheck deductions financed the Shook School until 1915 when Grundy County assumed that responsibility.

The Tennessee Coal, Iron and Railroad Company benefited enormously, as did Shook, from having inexpensive state prisoners, many of whom were Black, work company mines in Grundy County, thus depriving local men of their livelihood.

E. Gray Smith Packard Company

The Contributor 8/5/2020

In 1910, when he was eighteen years old, E. Gray Smith sold his first automobile. He sold it to the City of Nashville's engineering department for $3,000, "without the top and without the windshield." From 1910 to 1922, Smith handled the Winton line of automobiles. In 1924, after Winton quit manufacturing cars, Smith got the prestigious Packard automobile franchise in Nashville.

In 1957, when reflecting on the early days of automobiles in Nashville, Smith said, "we had auto shows [that were] a lot like the horse shows of today. We showed the cars in a ring at the state fair and at all the surrounding county fairs, too. Each car was graded on three points—the skill of the driver, the looks of the driver, and the car itself. We took special care to pick out a pretty gal who could drive well."

In 1928, Smith employed Carlton Brush Architects of Nashville to design a handsome building in the 2400 block of West End Avenue, in the middle of an exclusive residential neighborhood. In addition to the showroom that faced West End and across the street to Vanderbilt,

Smith had offices with glass partitions looking over the showroom, a large parts department, and a large service area. A second showroom, with large glass windows, faced Elliston Place. It was for used cars.

The new dealership's grand opening was on September 2, 1929. For the next two and one-half decades, Smith sold Packards from this location to many, perhaps most, of Nashville's wealthiest people. E. Gray Smith moved out of its 2400 West End Avenue building early in 1956 when Rich, Schwartz & Joseph relocated there.

In October 1955, Smith announced that he would open a new Packard agency, but that he chose not to disclose his plans at that time. Instead, he closed his Packard dealership the next year and became Nashville's Rolls Royce and Bentley dealer with his showroom and service department on Broadway.

After being in the automobile business for sixty-nine years, the E. Gray Smith business closed in 1979. After serving multiple uses, including that of a record store, the E. Gray Smith Building on West End was torn down in 2012 to make way for the seven-story Homewood Suites Hotel. In the hotel lobby, the owners display some of the handsome elements from the E. Gray Smith Dealership that stood there for twenty-eight years.

The old E. Gray
Smith Dealership
Courtesy of E. Gray
Smith Jr.

Mark Twain's Troubled Tennessee Roots

The Contributor 4/15/2020

Samuel Clemens, also known as Mark Twain, the great American humorist, was born in Florida, Missouri, on November 30, 1835. His life began there because his father Marshall Clemens's luck had run out in Tennessee. Born in Virginia, Marshall, who was named for U.S. Chief Justice John Marshall, left for Kentucky as a boy after his father's death. When his farm there failed, he and his wife, Jane, moved again, this time to Fentress County, Tennessee. There he became a self-educated lawyer and land speculator. Marshall began buying up land until he had more than 70,000 acres of virgin, yellow pine for which he had paid only $400. His hope was that a day would come when railroads, possibly from Cincinnati, would penetrate the mountains and haul timber from his land and make him and his family a fortune.

The Tennessee land investment only triggered the Clemens family's decline into poverty. This financial failure haunted Marshall and his family for decades and "fueled Sam Clemens' lifelong anxiety over money." Marshall, desperate for money, moved his family to Jamestown, Tennessee, where he opened a general store, above which his family lived.

The Clemens's first child, Pamela, was born there in 1827. One or two years later, Pleasant Hannibal was born in Jamestown. He lived only three weeks. In 1830, Margaret was born. Marshall Clemens began having headaches, which became increasingly severe. As his tiny store did not bring in sufficient income to feed his growing family,

Samuel Langhorne Clemens
Copyright by A. F. Bradley,
Library of Congress

he uprooted them again and in 1831 moved to a clearing in the woods at the confluence of three small streams. There, he built a cabin and opened a country store and became postmaster. He also tried to cultivate land so poor that it was almost unfarmable.

The financial crash of 1834 wiped out his credit. So, in 1835, he moved again, this time to Missouri, where his wife's sister lived. Her husband had written Marshall praising the country in these words, "It is the grandest country—the loveliest land—the purest atmosphere. I can't describe it; no pen could do it justice."

Soon after arrival in Missouri, Samuel Clemens was born. His father once again operated a general store with his brother-in-law, and began acquiring land, which was extremely fertile. He prospered somewhat and, in 1837, was named a judge in the Monroe County Court. Jane and Marshall ended up with seven children, too many to pay much attention to Samuel.

In 1838, the Clemenses moved once again, this time to Paris, Missouri, ten miles away, where there was a racetrack. Florida, Missouri had become a backwater town. A year later, Marshall saw an advertisement in a small newspaper saying that property was available in Hannibal, Missouri, some forty miles to the northeast. The Clemenses moved there, where Marshall, with the help of his oldest son, Orion, opened still another store, one the City of Hannibal didn't need. Marshall remained poor all his life which ended in 1847. His widow, Jane, lived a long life, dying at age eighty-seven. Their son, whose stage name was Mark Twain, went on to stardom.

Booker T. Washington and George Washington Carver

The Contributor 2/3/2021

Two of the greatest Alabamians of the years between the Civil War and World War II are buried side by side—not in Birmingham, Mobile, Montgomery, or Huntsville, but in the country town

Booker T. Washington (above)
and George Washington Carver
Photos by Frances Benjamin Johnston, Library of Congress

of Tuskegee at the Tuskegee Normal and Industrial Institute. They were Booker T. Washington, founder at age twenty-five of Tuskegee Normal and Industrial Institute, and its leading developer and his compatriot at the school, George Washington Carver. Both lived their adult lives in a segregated society in one of the poorest states in the Union where, between 1890 and 1915, Jim Crow laws discriminated violently against former slaves and their descendants.

Booker T. Washington, a brilliant rhetorician, was the leading voice of African Americans. He advocated getting along with White people and not confronting them, a controversial position. In the fall of 1896, Washington hired a brilliant graduate of Simpson College in Missouri to come to Tuskegee to take over a newly organized Agricultural Department. This man was George Washington Carver, whose profound knowledge of botany, agriculture, and soil economy enabled him to devise ways of helping the economically submerged South to better ways of living. Not content with mere scientific discovery for its own sake, he was passionately convinced that the results of research must be brought directly into the lives of the people. To this end, he traveled through the Deep South in a wagon filled with scientific exhibits of all kinds and with examples of aids to further better the lives of poor Americans, particularly Black people. On those weekend trips, he customarily met with Black farmers living way in the sticks. He urged them to quit relying on cotton as their cash crop and instead grow peanuts and sweet potatoes. He showed their wives how to pickle, can, and preserve vegetables and fruits. More than one Black Alabama farmer said Professor Carver "knows more than God does."

President Theodore Roosevelt knew and enormously respected both Booker T. Washington and George Washington Carver. Both men visited Roosevelt at the White House, and Roosevelt visited Tuskegee Institute. Secretary of Agriculture Henry C. Wallace was also an enormous supporter of both Booker T. Washington and George Washington Carver.

At age eighty-six, I probably will never see Tuskegee. I wish I had when I was younger and I urge you to do so. Should you go, you will also learn about the Tuskegee Airmen, who proved in Italy in World War II that Black men could become expert flyers.

Willis D. Weatherford

The Contributor 7/3/2019

In the June 9, 2019 issue of the *Tennessean,* I read that Vanderbilt had a commitment from a quarterback from Weatherford, Texas, to play football beginning in the fall of 2020. This reminded me of the first person from Weatherford to attend Vanderbilt.

Willis D. Weatherford, the sixth of seven children of Margaret Jane and Samuel Leonard Weatherford, was born in Weatherford, Texas, on December 1, 1875.

His parents' home consisted of two 18' by 18' rooms separated by a breezeway twelve feet wide. Mr. Weatherford was a cotton farmer and the brother of the man for whom Weatherford, Texas, was named. When Willis was seven years old, he entered the fourth grade in a public school. Until then, his mother had taught him at home. At age eight, he walked forward at the conclusion of a sermon, and told the family's Methodist minister he was ready to join the church. Willis had not informed his parents beforehand what he intended to do.

In 1888, the Weatherford family moved to town after Mr. Weatherford swapped his farm for a store and its stock of merchandise. While working for his father as cashier, Willis decided to continue his education. Weatherford College, a small local college that awarded BS and BA degrees, was his only option as money was scarce and he could save by living at home and by working part-time. While at Weatherford, Willis joined the student YMCA. After completing his sophomore year, his advisor told him he should study Greek. Willis told his parents and the family gathered on the front porch to consider the matter. His father thought it was not worthwhile. His mother listened and said nothing but later told Willis, "If you want to take Greek, take it." Willis graduated in 1894 as class valedictorian but with a backlog of debt he needed to repay before he could consider attending Vanderbilt, where he was set on going. So, he got a Texas teacher's certificate and taught at three different schools near Weatherford for three years.

In the spring of 1897, Willis was stricken with typhoid fever. He came close to death and suffered a partial loss of his eyesight. This was a huge problem because he needed to study literature, economics, and history in the summer in order to enter Vanderbilt the following fall as a junior. Willis got the summer work done only because his mother, who had a very limited education, read the material to him.

Willis achieved his goal of entering Vanderbilt in the fall of 1897 as a junior. His first year there, the tall, slim and ambitious Texan, who parted his brown hair in the middle and had blue eyes, lived in Wesley Hall, the School of Religion. He paid for his board by tending to the building's gas lighting system. During his second year at Vanderbilt, he got a job as an assistant instructor in the gymnasium under physical education professor Dr. J. T. Gwathmey. His salary there enabled him to move to a rooming house, where room and board cost $25 per month. Weatherford studied Greek, Southern literature, and mathematics at Vanderbilt, and won Phi Beta Kappa honors when he graduated in 1899 with a BA degree. After consulting with Vanderbilt chancellor, Dr. James H. Kirkland, who encouraged him,

Willis entered Vanderbilt Graduate School to work toward a PhD in philosophy.

Influenced by the famous YMCA secretary Fletcher Brockman, an 1891 Phi Beta Kappa graduate of Vanderbilt, Weatherford joined the Vanderbilt YMCA and became that organization's first graduate student president. Extremely popular with his fellow students, he was also president of the Graduate Club for three years.

The first day of Graduate School, Dr. Gwathmey, Willis's gymnasium instructor, told him that he was leaving Vanderbilt for a better-paying job in New York. Gwathmey thought Willis should take his job, so the two men went to see Chancellor Kirkland about the matter. Kirkland agreed and Weatherford was appointed director of the gymnasium.

Willis directed physical education at Vanderbilt for all three years he was in graduate school. In those years, all the male students, including football and baseball players, had to take physical education so Willis and his two assistants kept busy.

In 1900, the Nashville Athletic Club and the YMCA basketball teams challenged Vanderbilt to games. Until then, basketball had been an intramural affair at Vanderbilt with no coach. With a week's notice, Vanderbilt, coached by Weatherford, met the YMCA team on the Y court on December 15, 1900. Unaccustomed to the mesh wire backboards, the Commodores lost 22–19. Later that winter, Vanderbilt beat the YMCA team twice, 24–9 and 14–12. Weatherford coached the Vanderbilt basketball team for two more seasons. His 1902 team finished the season with a 5–2 record and outscored its opponents 158 to 125, and scoring an average of 23 points per game. Weatherford's experiences in physical education and coaching a college basketball team had a profound influence on him. He realized that there was a great need for educated men in the physical education field.

In March 1902, just before receiving his PhD, Weatherford received a telegram from John R. Mott, a future head of the International YMCA, asking him not to make a career decision until his assistant, Hans Anderson, could come to Nashville to talk. Surprised and flattered, Willis waited.

In April, Anderson came down and offered Weatherford a position as International YMCA Student Secretary for two hundred colleges in fourteen Southern and border states. Weatherford agreed to serve for three years, and a deal was struck.

In 1902, most of the colleges Willis visited were poor and conservative. College presidents saw Darwinism as a threat to their Christian beliefs. Weatherford was well prepared, however, to work with young college students. His religious convictions were sound, but he was willing to reach out to embrace new ideas. He also was personable and tireless. He visited seventy-five colleges a year, including every major university in the South. He started his talks by reading a short passage from a small New Testament that he carried in his pocket. He then launched into his subject without notes or repetition. A student later said, "He covered the South like a Paul Revere." A dynamic speaker

Willis D. Weatherford
Springfield College,
National YMCA Hall
of Fame

and a wise counselor, he became an intellectual and spiritual leader for hundreds, if not thousands, of students. One of the many influenced by Weatherford was Frank Porter Graham, who would become president of the University of North Carolina, United States Senator and a special mediator to the United Nations. Graham said this about Weatherford: "There were no bounds to Weatherford's energy and his devotion as he went from state to state and college to college. He had no patience with sloth, complacency, or low standards in religion, personal life, scholarship, athletics, and campus citizenship."

Because he lived in Nashville, Weatherford helped the Nashville Association when he could. In June 1904, he spoke to seventy members of the Boys' Hustling Club at the Y. In his inspirational talk, he encouraged the boys to meet "manfully and courageously the afflictions and temptations of life."

After his first year as YMCA secretary, Willis married Lula Belle Trawick, a small-boned brunette whom he met at Vanderbilt.

In 1904, he and Lula moved to live for a summer on a branch of the Swannanoa River in Western North Carolina. When he was a child, Willis's mother, who was born in Western North Carolina, had told him about her beloved mountains. When Willis attended a Student YMCA conference near Asheville in 1902, he fell in love with the country. At that time, student conferences in the summer were a big part of the student YMCA movement. As there was no permanent conference center, they met at a different place each summer, once at a hotel. At a summer conference held at the Asheville School for Boys, the legendary John R. Mott was the speaker. Willis told Mr. Mott of his dream of establishing a permanent YMCA Summer Conference Center. Mott encouraged him. Sometime later, a judge in Asheville, knowing of Weatherford's dream, told him about an ideal site for the conference center. It was in a mountainous area fifteen miles east of Asheville very close to where Weatherford and Lula Belle had spent their first summer.

In October 1906, Willis and a friend, Dr. A. L. Phillips, of the Presbyterian Sunday School Board in Richmond, visited the site. Pleased with it, they each borrowed $5,000 and bought the 952 acres for $11,500. They signed personal notes for the balance. Weatherford then launched a campaign to raise $50,000 to make the center a reality. The International YMCA in New York sent down a man to help him do something that most of Weatherford's friends thought impossible. Defying the enormous challenge, Weatherford ended up raising enough money to buy 1,585 acres of mountain land and began planning to erect a big, white-columned building to be called Lee Hall that he envisioned being the center of what would be named the Blue Ridge Assembly.

In June 1907, Weatherford received a terrible blow. His wife, Lula, died in childbirth. Their baby also died. Weatherford turned to incessant work as a refuge from the chaos and sorrow that followed his beloved wife's unexpected death, and that of the baby. Continuing to work as Student YMCA secretary and at Blue Ridge, Weatherford also kept in mind the inequities that people of color suffered. In April 1908 he brought seven leaders together in Atlanta, four Black leaders and three White, to discuss the racial situation and consider what they might do to help. John Hope, president of the Negro Atlanta Baptist College, and Dr. W. R. Lambuth, of the Southern Methodist Episcopal Church, were two of the men in attendance. Hope and Lambuth suggested that Weatherford write a book exposing the inequities. A direct result was that Willis researched and wrote a book on race relations, *Negro Life in the South*, that was published in 1910. It would be the first of five books he would write on race relations. In *Negro Life in the South,* Weatherford "called for an end to the stereotype of Negroes as shiftless and lazy." His second book, *Present Forces in Negro Progress*, dealt with Southern farm life and Negroes. In the book, he wrote, "The three arch enemies of Southern Farm Life today are tenant system, the one-crop system, and that form of isolation that cheats the rural dweller out of his birthright of culture, growth, and enjoyment."

By this time, everybody in the YMCA world knew about the offer that Chicago tycoon Julius Rosenwald, a Jewish man, had made in 1910 to give $25,000 toward construction of a YMCA for African Americans in any city that would match his gift with $75,000 over a period of five years. In making his offer, Rosenwald said he felt it "the duty of white people of this country, irrespective of their religious beliefs, to meet the needs of their neighbors." Weatherford, realizing that Rosenwald was on the same page he was on, went to see him. The result was that Rosenwald agreed to finance the project of sending *Present Forces in Negro Progress* to Southern farm demonstration agents.

In the summer of 1912, the Blue Ridge Assembly opened for its first season of youth conferences. Lee Hall, a white, frame structure with a broad front porch and eight stately columns, each three stories high, was finished and able to accommodate three hundred people. On the front porch, there were rocking chairs where guests could gaze at the mountain peaks across the valley. Weatherford had laid out the road to Lee Hall himself. On the first night of that first summer season, Weatherford spoke to the people in the main reception room. He would continue to do so for years. Weatherford, then only thirty-six years old, was Blue Ridge Assembly's first president and general director.

Willis was lonely as a bachelor. Fortunately, he found his second wife at Blue Ridge. Her name was Julia McRory, an Alabaman who had been secretary of the student YMCA at Winthrop College. They fell in love and married on May 27, 1914, at the home of the president of Winthrop College. Willis and Julia made their home at 2126 Blair Avenue in Nashville in the winters and in the summers from 1912 until 1944, at Blue Ridge. Some 150,000 young people, many personally selected by Weatherford, came to conferences at the Blue Ridge Center. They all came under the influence of Blue Ridge's founder and administrator. Theologians, teachers, and business leaders came each summer to speak. Blue Ridge was also one of the few places in the South where race relations could be openly discussed. African American leaders, such as Dr. Mordecai Johnson, president of Howard University in Washington, D.C., came to express their viewpoints. It is a wonder that, with such radical talk as went on at Blue Ridge, the Ku Klux Klan did not burn down Lee Hall.

One young White woman, who went to Blue Ridge from a town in Mississippi where there were three African Americans for each White person, told her class at Blue Ridge that she didn't think

Blue Ridge Assembly opened for its first season of youth conferences in the summer of 1912.   Blue Ridge Assembly website

Mississippi had a race problem, and said, "Everybody is happy." Everyone in the room just looked at her and it wasn't long before she realized how ignorant she was of the town she lived in. Many years later, she said, "Blue Ridge set me free in a way most people would find difficult to understand."

In 1915, William G. Frost, president of Berea College in Kentucky, came to Blue Ridge. At the end of his week-long stay, he told Weatherford, "You are doing the same thing here that we are at Berea: combining work and study. I want you to join the board of directors at Berea." The next year, Weatherford joined the Berea College Board and, for half a century, gave Berea his wise counsel. For thirty-five of those years, he was chairman of the board.

Weatherford continued as Student YMCA secretary for seventeen years. In that period, there was no college in the South with a graduate program to prepare young men to become YMCA secretaries. Only two colleges in the country had such programs—George Williams College in Chicago, and Springfield College in Massachusetts. As few young men from the South attended those colleges, there was a growing feeling that a permanent training school should be established in the South. Representatives of the state secretaries of the Southern YMCAs approached Weatherford about the idea and when he responded positively, asked him to consider being president of the school. When Weatherford was satisfied that he would have the support of YMCA secretaries in the South, he accepted. His idea was that the school should be a graduate school and be named the YMCA Graduate School. Because he and Mary lived in Nashville, where they were members of Belmont Methodist Church, and where he had gone to college, Willis felt that the school should be located there. Consequently, Weatherford met with officials at Vanderbilt and Peabody College. He told them his idea was to set up a four-quarter program of training with the summer quarter at Blue Ridge, and the three other quarters in Wesley Hall at Vanderbilt that was partially occupied by the struggling School of Religion. Chancellor Kirkland and President Bruce Payne of Peabody agreed to cooperate and they and Weatherford worked out a plan under which graduate students from Vanderbilt, Peabody, and the YMCA Graduate School would take half their courses in the institution in which they matriculated, but were free to take their other courses in either of the other schools. For example, someone working toward a master's degree in physical education at the YMCA Graduate School could take human anatomy courses at the Vanderbilt School of Medicine.

The YMCA Graduate School, chartered by the State of Tennessee to grant BA, MA, and DPE degrees, opened in 1919 in Wesley Hall on the Vanderbilt campus and remained there until 1927 when the school's handsome new building on 21st Avenue South across from Wesley Hall was built, thanks to a loan from Vanderbilt, who sold Weatherford the property just north of Peabody Demonstration School.

The YMCA Graduate School, also known as the Southern College of the YMCA, never had more than ten or twelve professors but their students had access to Vanderbilt's library. In retrospect, Weatherford wrote, "The arrangement was well-nigh perfect in its advantages to the YMCA." Several YMCA Graduate School faculty members went to Blue Ridge nearly every summer as did Weatherford's old associates at Vanderbilt—Oswald E. Brown, Dean of the Vanderbilt School of Religion, and Edwin Mims, head of the English Department. A member of the Vanderbilt Board of Trust later said that, had not the YMCA Graduate School taken over part of Wesley Hall, they probably would have voted to close the School of Religion.

The Graduate School DPE degree program required twelve quarters of work, three terms of the academic year were taken at the Graduate School while the summer term was held at the Blue Ridge Assembly at Black Mountain, North Carolina. The curriculum for the DPE degree consisted of 180 credit hours and was heavily slanted toward medical education. Some of the courses were bacteriology, venereal diseases, anthropometry, and physical examination, dermatology, anatomy, physiology, and mental and nervous diseases. These courses were taken at Vanderbilt. DPE students also took marching, gymnastic dancing, calisthenics, apparatus work, track, aquatics, football, basketball, and baseball at the YMCA Graduate School.

While running the YMCA Graduate School, Willis's wife, Julia, had contracted pleurisy and had to spend what turned out to be three years in a sanitarium in Colorado Springs. This left Willis to carry on in Nashville with their eight-year-old son, Willis Jr. The loneliness for all three was awful. Julia conquered pleurisy and returned home to be a mother and wife, and help her husband at the graduate school during the school year, and at Blue Ridge in the summers. Because the promised funding from Southern State YMCAs did not amount to much, Weatherford became a highly effective, one-man fundraising machine. His determination and personal conviction kept the school open in the face of criticism of him for being too liberal, as well as about the school's lack of money. He also endured the scorn of others who found his racial ideas intolerable. Weatherford's students, however, loved him. One said, "He was a spellbinder." Another said Weatherford "was spellbound, rapt, tireless, drawing superhuman strength from his spirituality."

By the 1920s, Dr. Weatherford was one of the most respected and effective YMCA leaders in the country. In 1923, when the International YMCA and the state associations were at odds, a constitutional convention was convened in Cleveland in October. On one side were advocates of "states' rights" while the other group favored a strong central control by the International YMCA. The gulf between the two was thought to be unbridgeable. Weatherford was one of three arbitrators asked to mediate the critical situation. After working three days and three nights, Weatherford presented their plan on the convention floor. Their proposal to combine a centralized organization with distributed responsibility was applauded. The plan was accepted by both sides and essentially became the structure, with modifications, under which the YMCA functions today.

Soon after the Cleveland Convention, Weatherford wrote *The Negro from Africa to America*, published in 1924 by George H. Doran Company. In 1965, Dr. George B. Tindall stated in his book, *Writing Southern History*, that *The Negro from Africa to America* "remains the best survey of [Black] history by a white writer." One of the highlights of Weatherford's years as Southern YMCA College president came in

Christmas at Lee Hall, YMCA Blue Ridge Assembly, 2021

1925 when the Laura Spelman Rockefeller Memorial Fund pledged $25,000 annually over a five-year period to the school.

After Weatherford had purchased the site on which to build his college building, he received an attractive offer to accept a position as a full professor and chair of Christian Methods at Yale University. After careful consideration, Weatherford turned down the offer because of the large opportunity he felt he had at the Southern YMCA College in Nashville into which he had poured so much energy. In 1925, there were twenty-five students at the YMCA Graduate School from ten states and one foreign country. Practically all of them taught Sunday school classes, and most performed social work in Nashville, including directing boys' activities at the Martha O'Bryan Settlement House and the Bertha Fensterwald Center.

In 1933, Julia became sick again. After hours of rest each day, she was able to come downstairs and even to participate to a limited degree in outside activities. While she was recovering, Dr. Weatherford had a hernia operation. One day soon after he returned home from the hospital, their son Willis Jr.'s dog, a big, friendly German Shepherd, began acting strangely. Their physician recommended that Julia and Willis Jr. take anti-rabies shots. Julia did so only on the urging of her husband

and physician. After her thirteenth shot, she lost consciousness and was rushed to the hospital. After hovering between life and death, she regained consciousness, but was paralyzed from the waist down. Julia recovered some use of her upper body and legs, but that proved temporary and she remained partially paralyzed for the remaining twenty-four years of her life. For the next three years Weatherford spent time and money trying to find a cure for his wife. He also struggled to raise funds for the YMCA Graduate School.

By 1935, the YMCA Graduate School was unable to pay interest on its debt to Vanderbilt. Its impending demise would cause great problems for Vanderbilt because university students used the Graduate School gym and swimming pool and received instruction from three Graduate School faculty members at $20 per student. For almost a year, Weatherford and Chancellor Kirkland discussed proposals for some kind of merger. Weatherford was willing to surrender the building to Vanderbilt if the university would assume the graduate school's $166,000 debt, and if he could retain a right to later repurchase the building. Vanderbilt considered accepting this, but their attorney found that a second mortgage precluded a clear title. Finally, in 1936, Weatherford gave up and sought foreclosure. He managed to retire the second mortgage and late that year turned the property over to Vanderbilt for about $176,000 of cancelled debt.

Vanderbilt renamed the building Wesley Hall after the original Wesley Hall that burned in 1932, and moved the School of Religion there. This seemed appropriate since so many graduates of the School of Religion went into YMCA work.

The loss of the YMCA Graduate School was a serious blow to the entire YMCA movement as the school had been a matter of pride to the national Y. A few years later, it was found that 80 percent of all the student YMCA secretaries in Southern colleges and universities were graduates of the YMCA Graduate School. Historian C. Howard Hopkins concluded in 1951 that the YMCA Graduate School "was the most challenging and possessed the greatest potential of the several professional educational ventures attempted by the Association." In 1968, he had not changed his mind. That year, Hopkins wrote that the

YMCA Graduate School "always seemed to me to be a statesman-like effort of much greater significance than it has been accorded."

After the Graduate School closed, Dr. Thomas Elsa Jones, president of Fisk University and a Northern-born, White Quaker, invited Dr. Weatherford to join the Fisk faculty. The challenge of working with Black students was irresistible. Weatherford accepted. A puzzled department head at Vanderbilt asked him why he wanted to teach at Fisk. Weatherford replied, "Because I've been interested in the race question for a long time and this is a chance to see what I can do about it." The man turned away and said, "Queer the choices some people make."

Weatherford's new position at Fisk was Chairman of the Department of Religion and Philosophy. He also prepared and introduced an introductory course in the humanities, the first such course taught at Fisk. In time, it became a required course for sophomores. While teaching at Fisk, Weatherford continued to run Blue Ridge during the summers and to participate as a trustee at Berea and help the interracial Commission (ACIPCO) that he helped found.

In 1940, he and Julia built a home they called "Far Horizons," on a steep ridge, called Overlook, behind the Blue Ridge Center. They used native materials from 185 acres they owned there, including river-worn stone and poplar logs. Far Horizons became their permanent home. From their mountain home, at an elevation of 3,200 feet, they could see twenty peaks that rose 5,000 feet or higher. In 1943, a committee representing the Southern YMCAs came to see Weatherford to ask him to consider turning the Blue Ridge property over to the Southern associations. Weatherford welcomed the suggestion and agreed to do so, with two stipulations. The YMCA would have to agree to raise the money to pay off his $74,000 indebtedness and make improvements on the building. The second stipulation was that the Southern associations would continue to use Blue Ridge as a religious training center for the young people of the South. This came about and, in 1944, he severed his official ties with the center. Two years later, at age seventy, Weatherford resigned from the faculty at Fisk, having been there ten years.

Two years later, Berea invited Weatherford to join their faculty in a special capacity. He did so and divided his time between Berea and helping his ailing wife in efforts that were described as "heroic." One of his major responsibilities at Berea was to find prospective students. During the winters, he would go out into the snow-covered valleys and coves of East Kentucky looking for students. With the school approaching its 100th anniversary in 1955, Weatherford proposed to the Berea Board of Trustees that they underwrite a drama that would help the mountain people know their heritage and, indirectly, build a constituency of people who knew about Berea and its purpose. The board agreed, and in the summer of 1955 "Wilderness Road" opened in the handsome Indian Fort Theater three miles from the Berea campus. The trustees had by then invested $250,000 in the project. During that summer, applications to Berea increased by over 500. "Wilderness Road" ran for four summers and drew 160,000 in paid attendance, but still lost $25,000. Despite the fact that visitors coming to the drama often stayed at the college-owned Boone Tavern, one year nearly doubling the inn's summer revenue, the trustees voted to close the drama. Weatherford was disappointed but moved on.

Julia Weatherford suffered a heart attack in September 1957 and died a few weeks later. She had lived to see one of her five grandchildren, the oldest of four daughters and one son of their son, Willis Jr., and his wife, Anne. Her most cherished dream of having a loving family for her son was realized.

In March 1960, Willis D. Weatherford suffered a slight stroke. He hardly noticed and kept working on his latest book, *The Southern Appalachian Region: A Survey*. Published by the University of Kentucky Press in 1962, it was the story of many men and women, boys and girls that he had met in many decades of walking through the hills and hollows of Appalachia.

On Willis Weatherford's 90th birthday in 1965, Dr. Alexander Heard, the brilliant young chancellor of Vanderbilt, said of him, "His career has been long. His lifetime of labor for social justice, wider economic horizons, and better conditions of life for the people of our section has won enduring fame for him and lasting pride for his alma mater."

On December 1, 1965, the Appalachian Regional Commission in Washington drafted a resolution congratulating Weatherford on his ninety years and pointing out that "his ideas, his energy and his leadership have greatly aided in focusing national concern and attention on the region which now has been translated into action in the Appalachian Regional Development Act of 1965 and this Commission's current program to develop the Appalachian Region." Willis D. Weatherford died in 1970 in his 95th year, having accomplished more after he turned eighty than most men do in a lifetime.

William C. Weaver Jr. (1912–1979)

The Contributor 8/28/2019

William C. "Bill" Weaver Jr. was born October 10, 1912, at "Seven Oaks," the home of his parents, Irene Morgan and William C. "Will" Weaver, five miles from Nashville on Murfreesboro Road. As a little boy, Bill and his sister, Henriette, only fourteen months older, had more freedom than most city children as there was very little traffic on the still unpaved Murfreesboro Road. Everybody in the neighborhood knew, were fond of, and protective of the Weaver children. Bill Weaver's aunt, Edna Harris, lived next door at "Kingsley," the magnificent antebellum home designed by William Strickland, the architect for the Tennessee State Capitol.

Across the road from Kingsley stood "Colemere," the home of Bill's uncle, Dempsey Weaver, and his wife, Anna Cole Weaver. Toward town and a little below and across the road from Seven Oaks was Arlington Methodist Church, where the Weavers and Harrises were members. About a mile away toward town was Herschel Gower's general store, where Mr. and Mrs. Weaver regularly bought gas or staple items. Further out the highway was Mr. McMahon's store and the Tennessee Asylum for the Insane that had been administered by Mr. Weaver's great-grandfather, Dr. William Archer Cheatham, in the 1850s.

Each summer when school was out, Bill and Henriette looked forward to going by train and later by automobile with their grandparents or parents to the Morgan family summer home, "Restover," in the Monteagle Sunday School Assembly in Monteagle, Tennessee. Matilda Evans Morgan, Bill's grandmother, built the cottage in 1900 with money she inherited from an uncle. Her father-in-law, Dr. William Henry Morgan, spent one summer there before his death in 1901. Her husband—Dr. Morgan's son, Dr. Henry William Morgan, the first graduate of Vanderbilt Medical School—came on weekends until his death in 1920. Their five children, including Bill's mother, Irene Morgan Weaver, and his uncle, Dr. Walter McNairy Morgan, spent part of their summers there, as did various aunts and uncles and first cousins. When Bill's uncle Dr. Walter Morgan was a teenager, he worked various jobs at the Assembly, and was the best tennis player on the grounds. Walter was so good that he won the Tennessee State Tennis Singles Championship twice.

When Bill was a teenager, he always got a job at Monteagle within a day or two of arrival. First, he was a pin boy at the bowling alley and later worked at the front gate. In his spare time, he played tennis on the assembly courts or swam in the swimming pool. He and Henriette almost never took hikes outside the assembly grounds because their parents said the woods were full of moonshiners. Bill had a first cousin, Jean Ewing, who often was at Restover when he was. Bill loved to tease and scare her by jumping out at her in disguise. He also made a habit of walking across the bridges on the rail ignoring Jean's plea to "get down, Bill, get down!"

The Weavers also had a clay tennis court behind their house on Murfreesboro Road. There, and at Monteagle, Bill gained a lifelong love for the game. His father, Mr. Will Weaver, drove to town every day to his wholesale hardware and appliance business—McWhirter, Weaver & Company—on Second Avenue North. When the children were old enough to go to school, they rode to town with him or with the Dempsey Weavers' chauffeur to Peabody Demonstration School, where Bill and Henriette started school together in the first grade. Bill, who was tall and thin, played football and basketball at Peabody. He and Henriette graduated in 1930. Bill entered Vanderbilt that fall but, with the Depression in full swing, dropped out in 1932 to go to work at his father's business. His first job was selling refrigerators door to door that summer.

Bill invited his girlfriend, Elizabeth Craig, of Nashville, to the Monteagle Assembly for a few days. Elizabeth, who had just completed her freshman year at Smith College, came to the mountain aware that the Smith College Foundation, to which she contributed $10 annually, supported the nearby Highlander Folk School. She told Bill she would like to see the place. Bill agreed to drive her over there, but said they couldn't get in. Elizabeth bet him that they could. At Highlander, Elizabeth introduced herself and Bill to Myles Horton, the director, and told him that she attended Smith College. Horton immediately picked up on the connection and graciously took them on a tour of the facilities. At the library, the only one then open to the public in Grundy County, Bill noticed that many of the books were related to the labor movement. As they walked back to Bill's car, he said, "Let's get the hell out of here before this place explodes." Bill also paid off the bet he lost to Elizabeth.

A natural salesman and businessman, Bill became treasurer and, after his father died in 1943, president and chairman of the board of

Bill Weaver, behind Jesse E. Wills, attends a Cheekwood exhibit sponsored by National Life and WSM in 1971.
Collection of Ridley Wills II

McWhirter, Weaver & Company. Bill married Elizabeth Craig, the oldest daughter of Mr. and Mrs. Edwin W. Craig, May 15, 1940, at Nashville's West End United Methodist Church. When he went up to National Life to ask Mr. Craig for Elizabeth's hand in marriage, Mr. Craig, then Executive Vice President of the company, gave the wedding his blessing. He also encouraged his future son-in-law to join National Life. Mr. Craig already knew Bill was charismatic and business-smart.

Bill Weaver joined the life insurance company in 1940, becoming a supervisor in the Mortgage Loan Division of the Investment Department. Every day, after working a full day at National Life, he went down to McWhirter Weaver and put in a couple of hours there.

Bill left National Life on a leave of absence in May 1944, a month before their daughter, Becky, was born, to join the U.S. Army as an enlisted man. He had tried to get a commission but at 6'5" tall and color blind, he was rejected.

In 1946, Bill returned to National Life's Mortgage Loan Division and became assistant manager of the division the next year. By then, his children, Bill Weaver III, born March 18, 1941, and Becky, three years younger, spent portions of their summers at Restover, where their grandmother Irene Morgan Weaver, made her home for five months of the year. Bill would drive up for weekends where he played tennis on the same courts where his uncle Walter Morgan had once been king. Bill did not accept opportunities to become a board member because he had heard stories of his grandmother, Matilda Morgan, stretching out on a sofa at Restover taking spirits of ammonia, after returning to her cottage from long, tedious, and often contentious board meetings. Besides, Bill came to Monteagle to relax after busy weeks in the business world. In 1957, Bill's mother, Irene Morgan Weaver, died, only three days after leaving the mountain. She too had served on the assembly board for several terms. Money given to the assembly in her memory, supplemented by monetary gifts from Bill and his sister, Henriette Weaver Jackson, was used to finance the first endowed memorial Sunday sermon named in Mrs. Weaver's memory and so initiated the present fully endowed sermon program. Monteagle stalwart, Cornelia Keeble Ewing, suggested designating gifts for this worthy project.

Bill Weaver Jr. went on to successively become manager of National Life's Real Estate and Mortgage Loan Department (1953), financial vice president (1963), senior vice president (1964), executive vice president (1967), and president (1969). In 1972 he was named Chairman of the Board and chief executive officer of NLT the following year.

During his time as CEO of National Life, the company climbed to become the 19th largest life insurance company in the country and sixth largest among stock companies. Bill also served on the boards of Third National Bank, Third National Corporation, and Hospital Corporation of America. He was also on the advisory board of Ralston Purina Company and developed, with a partner, Nashville's Green Hills Shopping Center.

Bill Weaver Jr. retired from NLT and WSM, where he was Chairman of the Board, in 1977. In the latter capacity, he oversaw the completion of Opryland USA and the move of the world-famous Grand Ole Opry to the new quarters at Opryland. Two years later, at age sixty-six, Bill Weaver Jr., whose influence was felt in nearly all facets of Nashville life, died of cancer. The *Nashville Tennessean* spoke of his community leadership and also of his "great personal charm and natural warmth."

In an editorial titled "Mr. Weaver Left Region a Richer, Better Place," Wayne Whitt, the newspaper's managing editor, wrote that Bill Weaver "had an interest in all people, regardless of wealth or station. He was a lively companion, on a duck hunt, or at a luncheon. He had awareness, curiosity and a zest for life and challenge." In 1980, three tennis courts at the Monteagle Sunday School Assembly were named for Bill Weaver Jr. whose greatest pleasure at the assembly was to find a doubles partner who could help him beat his son, Bill Weaver III, and Bill's wife, Nicky. Fiercely competitive, Bill gave no quarter on the court to anyone, including Bill and Nicky, or his daughter Becky, all of whom he loved dearly.

Leaving a Job with a Family Legacy Can Be a Big Decision

Ridley Wills talks about how he made one of the biggest choices of his life.

The Contributor 7/14/2021

By the time American General announced its acquisition of NLT on November 4, 1982, I had decided to stay with American General long enough to determine if I felt comfortable working for that company. As I was then chairing National Life's annual United Way campaign, I did not want to leave in the midst of the campaign, because, without leadership, I thought the campaign might flounder. That year, the combined employee contribution from L&C and National Life employees to the United Way was $288,380. Five years after the merger, in the 1987–88 United Way campaign, American General home office employees gave $172,578, a 30 percent decrease over five years. For a number of years before the takeover, National Life had raised more money for the United Way than any company in Nashville. In 1978, I was chairman of Nashville's United Way Campaign.

Very quickly following the NLT-AG merger, two things happened that told me I probably should resign from American General. In 1982, I had been on the board of directors of National Life for six years. With the takeover, the board's name was changed to the American General Life and Accident Insurance Company Board. One day, when the board was to meet, I got a phone call from the secretary of one of the executive officers telling me that I did not need to attend the meeting. When I asked her why, she said I was no longer on the board. I was taken aback at the insensitive manner in which AG's executive management handled my dismissal.

One of the innovations that American General brought to the National Life office staff of well over 1,000 people, was to introduce a management plan called Model-Netics that every home office employee was expected to learn. Model-Netics consisted of 50 or more models, which collectively gave the philosophy of the company. Two of the models that I remember were, "If you are on a northbound train and want to go south, you should get off the train." The other was, "the appropriate amount of resources to accomplish a job is the minimum resource needed to accomplish the task."

American General needed someone to teach the first Model-Netics class to National Life employees. To do so, that person would need to go to Sacramento, California, where Harold Hook, American General's CEO, had a brother who taught the class to various American General company employees. I volunteered to be that person, was accepted, and went to Sacramento for a week to learn how to teach the class at National Life. There I also learned that Harold Hook, the company's CEO, owned Model-Netics and profited by selling it to his companies.

I volunteered to teach the first class at National Life because, if I did leave the company's employment, I thought I would like to teach Nashville history as an ad hoc professor at an educational institution. So I taught the first class at National Life. In December 1982, two decisions I made were overturned, I suppose by H. J. Bremermann Jr., the newly appointed CEO of American General Life and Accident Insurance Company of Tennessee. In December of each year, I evaluated the written goals of the department heads reporting to me. Four of those departments paid claims—death claims, policy loans, cash surrenders, and sick and accident claims. I gave each of these department heads a goal to pay claims as quickly as they could. The faster their employees paid claims, the larger the annual bonus I gave them. I did this because I knew that American General policyowners, many of whom were African Americans, were relatively poor. I knew that they needed the money. I also knew that, when my grandfather, Ridley Wills, and Neely Craig founded National Life in 1901, they decided that if they were good to their policyowners who then were all Black, everyone else would do just fine. Accordingly, Neely and Ridley put a sign in the agent's room of every district office that read as follows:

Pay all just claims promptly and pleasantly;
Reject all unjust claims firmly but pleasantly.
If there is any doubt, give the policy owner
the benefit of the doubt.

Soon after giving bonuses in December 1982, I received word to quit paying claims so promptly. This was a shock and a second sign that I was on a "train going north while I wanted to go south." The other blow came when I recommended salary increases for my department heads. At about the same time, the underwriting departments of Life and Casualty and National Life were housed side by side in what had recently been the NLT Tower but were still operating separately. Jack Gwaltney headed the National Life Underwriting Department while Clark Hutton headed the smaller Life and Casualty Underwriting Department. Jack was making $65,000 a year while Clark, who was within a year of retirement, made $35,000 annually. I did not recommend a salary increase that year for Jack, but recommended a modest cost of living increase for Clark. My recommendation for Clark was turned down, assumingly by the CEO.

American General announced at about the beginning of 1983 that it would sell WSM, the Grand Ole Opry, and the Opryland Theme Park. Soon thereafter, I was invited by Walter Robinson, the former CEO of NLT, to join a group he headed to buy these companies. I felt honored to have been asked to become a minor member of the group, which made an offer of between $200 million and $300 million for the companies to be sold. On March 16, 1983, American General announced that it would shop around for a larger offer.

On July 1, 1983, Gaylord Broadcasting signed a letter of intent to buy the Opryland properties for $270 million. This ended the attempt by the group of us, headed by Walter Robinson Jr., to acquire it.

Sometime in the autumn or early fall, Harold Hook Jr. asked me to fly to Houston and spend a weekend with him on his ranch. I had no clue why he wanted me to do this and assumed he simply wanted to get to know me better, as I was a senior officer. I knew I was not in contention for a promotion to executive vice-president because AG had just promoted Bob Devlin, William Darragh Jr., and Neil Anderson to the three executive vice-president slots that were open. Devlin's office, until his promotion, was next to mine. We were jointly responsible for merging the home office operations of quite a few National Life and Life & Casualty departments. I had learned that Bob never seemed to write anything down and that he talked daily with Hook by long distance. I figured he was Hook's spy in Nashville. So, his promotion came as no surprise.

By the autumn of 1983, I decided to quit. A couple of hours after submitting my written resignation, I saw Bremermann, the CEO, downtown at lunch time. He stopped and said something to the effect that he knew I would enjoy being in Texas with Harold Hook. I told him that I was not going to Texas and had just submitted my letter of resignation. He seemed disappointed. Bremermann was later fired by Hook.

Ridley Wills II receives his 25th anniversary pin from Carroll Shanks, September 1983   Collection of Ridley Wills II

Leaving American General, effective October 21, 1983, was my second-best decision ever. After doing so, to my surprise, I was elected to the Vanderbilt University Board of Trust when I didn't even have a job, and chaired MBA's Board of Trustees for nine years, chairing the committees that employed two outstanding headmasters, Douglas Paschal and Brad Gioia. I have since 1990 written and published thirty books and three booklets, and was given in May 2016 an honorary PhD by the University of the South for being one of Tennessee's foremost historians. I also taught Nashville history as an ad hoc professor at Belmont University for fifteen or more years, and in March 2022, I was inducted in the Southeast United States YMCA Hall of Fame in Black Mountain, North Carolina.

Ann Potter Wilson, David K. Wilson's first wife, on hearing that I had left American General, told Pat, "I never thought Ridley was suited to be in the life insurance business."

What I know for certain is that I have received much enjoyment and satisfaction in my life since leaving American General. I made the right decision.

[Jen A's response to Ridley's "Nashville History Corner" article concerning his decision to leave American General in 1983.]

Hey Ridley!

I've wanted to write for some time to tell you how much I genuinely appreciate the articles you place in *The Contributor*. But after reading your piece in the last issue, I decided I shouldn't wait any longer. Over the past year we've all had a chance to reflect and look critically at our lives. You write masterfully about a decision you made long ago that changed the trajectory of your life and the lives of your family. But quite honestly, I don't think you're giving yourself enough credit.

I wasn't born in Nashville. I wandered into town broken and desperate about ten years ago. And while I wouldn't exactly say I've thrived, thanks in large measure to your illuminating histories of the people, places, and events that made Nashville your family's home, I've found my home. It's always refreshing to read the true history of a place delivered without pretense. Few writers can reach past the hype to the truth as you do so elegantly.

Everyone has to make tough choices in life. Probably no one knows that better than *The Contributor* vendors. Every one of us has come to a place where we are pretty much out of options. And when we got to that dark, frightening place, there was your son, Tom, eager and willing to take us by the hand. He gives us purpose and a way up from the very bottom of the ladder. He's both saved and changed lives in his own special creative way. Do you think the son of a driven-to-succeed insurance executive would have done that? I wonder.

I guess what I'm trying to say is I think you've done alright for yourself and your family, Ridley. Your work is a great credit to the place you and generations of your family before you have called home. You've made me know and understand how Nashville came to be the quirky, wonderful town it is. I'm grateful to call the Nashville of Ridley Wills II and his family my home.

Private Buildings

Jackson Building

The Contributor 5/2/2016

Now that the 45-story 505 Tower is rising on the southwest corner of Fifth Avenue North and Church Street, it seems appropriate to look back 123 years and see what was there in 1893. Then, several small buildings occupied the site. But that was about to change.

In the early 1890s, Gen. William Hicks "Billy" Jackson sold part of his interest in the Belle Meade Stud to Richard Coker, a New York politician. With those funds and his other assets and those of his brother, Howell E. Jackson—then a newly appointed associate justice on the Supreme Court of the United States—Billy and Howell decided to build a modern, fireproof office/apartment building on Church Street just across Summer Street from the First Presbyterian Church.

In speaking of their plans to the editor of the *Confederate Veteran*, Gen. Jackson said, "There may be larger buildings in other cities, but there is no building better furnished than this will be." The *Confederate Veteran* editor wrote "there are four hundred tons of steel in the structure of the building" and that "the first story is built of what is known as limestone from his Belle Meade quarry. The other floors will be built of fire brick and terra cotta and cut stone trimmings, to be the same color as the stone of the first story. The steel frame to the fourth story is up, and the stone part of the wall is nearly completed. The building will contain a nine-foot basement, seven stories, and a roof garden lighted by electricity. The garden will not be for the public but for the Jacksons and their friends, and its management will be regulated for them. All Nashville is proud of the magnificent structure."

Jackson Building
Collection of
Ridley Wills II

The fireproof Jackson Building, the tallest structure in the city, rose 120 feet above ground level. When completed in 1895, it cost $157,091.83. The first floor contained several stores facing Church Street and one store facing Summer. The second through the fourth floors held offices while the fifth through seventh floors were designed for apartments.

For the first forty some-odd years of the twentieth century, my grandfather, Dr. Matthew G. Buckner, Justice Jackson's son-in-law, practiced medicine from his office in the Jackson Building, which was managed for many of those years by his brother-in-law, Harding A. Jackson.

When I was a boy in the 1940s, my dentist, Dr. Walter Morgan, practiced dentistry there. I remember looking across Church Street from his dental chair and counting brick in the Lebeck Building while he drilled away.

One of Dr. Buckner's worst days came in 1941 when he walked outside one afternoon to drive home and noticed someone on a Coca-Cola crate preaching to a crowd. Curious to see what it was all about, Dr. Bucker peered in and, to his horror, realized it was his grandson, Stuart Ragland Jr., a senior at MBA, who was living with the Buckners.

Stuart was extolling the virtues of Adolph Hitler. Later, Stuart became a naval pilot in World War II.

In 1944, Cain-Sloan Company obtained a 99-year lease on the Jackson Building, which was demolished in the spring of 1949 to make way for Cain-Sloan's new department store and a parking garage. Cain-Sloan built the building and operated it until July 1987 when it was vacated.

On July 2, 1993, Tony Giarratana purchased the former Cain-Sloan building for $2 million and also land beneath it from forty Harding-Jackson family heirs. He sold the entire package to Allright Parking Inc. of Houston, retaining an exclusive right to repurchase the property.

The Cain-Sloan building was razed to make way for a parking lot. The parking lot was later re-purchased by Giarratana, who announced in December 2014 that he would build a 60-story residential high-rise on the site. Those plans were scaled back to a 45-story high-rise with 500 multi-family units. Named the "505 Tower," it is well underway as is an MDHA 973-space parking garage immediately behind the Tower.

Life & Casualty Tower

The Contributor 7/20/2015

The Life & Casualty Tower, now known as the L&C Tower, was Nashville's first post–World War II skyscraper. It was twice as tall as Nashville's second tallest building, the 15-story American Trust Building built in 1926 at 235 Third Avenue North.

L&C Tower remains a wonderful example of a regional interpretation of international style. On its top, Edwin Keeble, the building's architect, installed neon L&C letters that changed colors to tell Nashvillians the local weather forecast: red meant rain or snow, blue meant clear or sunny, and pink designated a cloudy day. The L&C Tower, which has a four-story lobby, dominated the city's skyline for many years and remains as one of Nashville's great buildings of the twentieth century.

The Arcade

The Contributor 1/25/2016

In 1902 and 1903, the Edgefield and Nashville Manufacturing Company erected an arcade between Cherry and Summer streets halfway between Church and Union streets in downtown Nashville.

The architect for the 360-foot-long and 75-foot-wide building was the firm of Thompson, Gibel and Asmus. The Arcade has two tiers of shops under a gabled glass roof. In 1903, there were 53 businesses in the building that covers almost an acre.

When the Arcade opened on May 20, 1903, more than 40,000 people were said to have visited it. They witnessed patriotic demonstrations and heard a band playing from the balcony. Dan Buntin, the owner of the Arcade, got the idea of building it from an arcade he saw in Milan, Italy.

Although arcades were relatively common in the United States at the beginning of the twentieth century, there are relatively few today. Fortunately, one of the surviving arcades is in the heart of downtown Nashville, still accessed from Fourth and John Lewis Way or from an alley that runs through the middle of the Arcade between Church and Union Streets. Today, the Arcade contains a U.S. Post Office, a number of art studios, and quite a few restaurants.

Postcard view of the Arcade on opening day in 1903

Collection of Ridley Wills II

Radio Station

WSM

The Contributor 10/5/2015

In about 1921, Edwin Craig, manager of National Life and Accident Insurance Company's Ordinary Department, began bugging his father, C. A. Craig, president of the company, and two other executive officers, Ridley Wills, and C. Runcie Clements, about establishing a radio station to support the company's agents, spread out over twenty-one states. The three company founders were dubious but Edwin was persistent, having been caught up in the national mania for broadcasting. Finally, in February 1923, they gave in. It took Edwin, however, until April 7, 1925, to work out a deal to transfer the broadcasting license of WOAN in Lawrenceburg to National Life. Craig then ordered a 1,000-watt transmitter from Western Electric, which made the new National Life station and WSB in Atlanta the only two stations with that much power.

WSM went on the air October, 5, 1925. Its call letters "WSM" stood for "We Shield Millions." The station's original format was band music, featuring the orchestras of Frances Craig and Beasley Smith, lectures, and light classical music. George D. Hay, the "solemn Old Judge," became WSM's program director, and Jack DeWitt, at age nineteen, the station's chief engineer. Soon thereafter, WSM launched a Saturday night country music program that became the Grand Ole Opry. Dr. Humphrey Bates and his Possum Hunters were the first to perform country music on the station. The biggest star in the late 1920s was Uncle Dave Macon, the "Dixie Dewdrop." In 1927, WSM's power was increased to 5,000 watts. Five years later, the company was awarded a clear channel of 650 kilowatts and approved to increase its watts from 5,000 to 50,000. In preparation for this, National Life built a new vertical-type radio tower on Concord Road in Brentwood that was 878 feet tall, the tallest radio tower in the United States.

On October 14, 1940, a half-hour segment of the Grand Ole Opry, sponsored by Prince Albert Smoking Tobacco, went national on NBC. George Hay announced the segment while Roy Acuff was the star. By then, the Grand Ole Opry was the core of WSM's programming. The clear-channel station, known as the "Air Castle of the South," had an audience, particularly on Saturday nights, that spanned much of the eastern half of the United States. In 1943, *Variety Magazine*, the industry's leading trade paper, wrote, "WSM produces and presents more commercial and sustaining NBC shows than any other operation in the United States outside of New York, Chicago, and Hollywood." Jack Stapp, WSM's ambitious program director during the 1940s and 1950s, cultivated stars Cousin Minnie Pearl, Pee Wee King, Roy Acuff, and Snooky Lanson. When Acuff left the show in 1946, Red Foley stepped into his shoes as the anchor for the Prince Albert Opry feed and quickly became one of the best-known hillbilly and folk music vocalists in the country. Fortunately, Acuff returned to WSM. His trademark song, so often sung on the Grand Ole Opry, was "The Great Speckled Bird." In the summer of 1947, WSM became the first Nashville station to obtain a television license.

In 1949, WSM invited Hank Williams, one of the most troubled country singers the country had ever seen, to join the Opry. He did, but his heavy drinking and rebellious ways immediately landed him in trouble. Exasperated, WSM management put down an ultimatum: Unless he made his next Opry appearance on Saturday night, August 9, 1952, he would be fired. Williams never showed up and was fired. He died December 30, 1952, while being chauffeured from Knoxville to an engagement in Ohio.

WSM-TV came on the air August 13, 1950. Larry Munson, Nashville's most popular sports broadcaster, moved to WSM where he became the play-by-play voice of both the Nashville Vols and the Vanderbilt Commodores. Munson went on to a storied career as the voice of the University of Georgia football and basketball teams.

The next big innovation at WSM was the development and growth of FM radio. To enter the market, WSM bought WLWM-FM in 1968 and changed its call letters to WSM-FM. FM's superior sound quality caused FM stations to spring up everywhere and it would not be too long before a majority of radio listeners preferred listening to FM stations.

Construction of a new Opry House began in November 1971, with the grand opening on March 16, 1974. The building immediately

Located in Nashville, WSM radio tower, at 878 feet, was America's tallest.
Collection of Ridley Wills II

became the centerpiece of NLT Corporation's $43 million, 369-acre Opryland entertainment-recreation complex.

In the 1970s, Pat Sajak, Dan Miller, and Jud Collins were three of WSM's top radio and television performers. For decades WSM dominated the nightly news ratings with *The Scene at Six* and *The Scene at Ten*. Nashville television's first news anchor, Teddy Bart, was another popular talk show host at WSM. Later, Bill Hall was a tremendously popular weatherman. The Channel 4 team in 1984 consisted of Dan Miller (news), Demetria Kalodimos (news), Bill Hall (weather) and Charlie McAlexander (sports).

Along the street railroad on August 10, 1893, a crowd makes a run on Fourth National Bank on College Street in Nashville.
Collection of Ridley Wills II

Railroads

Nashville Boasted
the Finest Street Railroad in the South

The Contributor 3/16/2015

The various Nashville street railroad systems were combined in a unified system under the Tennessee Electric Street Power Company in 1915. Streetcars from all lines ran through a transfer station which stood a half block north of Deaderick between Third and Fourth Avenues North. Earlier, in 1907, W. O. Thomas bragged in the *Taylor-Trotwood Magazine* that "Nashville has the finest street railroad system in the South."

Mountain Goat Depot
at Monteagle, Tennessee (ca. 1910)

The Contributor 8/18/2021

In 1910, the Tracy City Branch passenger train No. 121, known as the Mountain Goat, stopped at Monteagle daily. It came up the mountain daily from Cowan with earlier stops at St. Mary's, Sewanee, and St. Andrews before reaching Monteagle. The grade up the mountain was steep, the road bed rough and the turns sharp. There was a

"Mountain Goat" steam engine was actually the Tracy City Branch passenger train number 121.

baggage car and usually three or four passenger cars. The engine puffed and popped off steam as it climbed. Cinders rained on top of the cars like sleet and, if you stuck your head out of the window, you got a faceful. The cars rattled and shook so you could not stand in the aisle. The wheels squeaked and groaned. On the sharp curves, you could see the engineer and fireman working in the cab. These were the memories of Dr. Edwin K. Provost, who first came to Monteagle by train when he was six months old.

Dr. Provost recalled in 1982 that the train, in 1910, left Nashville at 8 a.m. and arrived at Cowan at 12:30 p.m. "There was excitement on getting aboard [in Nashville] as friends from Memphis, Mississippi, and Arkansas were already on the train," he wrote. "We went through Smyrna, Murfreesboro, Wartrace, Bell Buckle, Tullahoma, and Decherd to Cowan. The train stopped there and the cars which were going up the mountain were uncoupled and the train went on to Chattanooga."

Across the tracks in Cowan was the two-story Franklin House Hotel. "When the train arrived, a man with a white jacket and white chef's hat walked up and down the hotel porch ringing a bell," Provost wrote. "You could eat at the Franklin House or the hotel could send a box lunch to the train. Quite a number had lunch baskets that they brought with them. Shortly, after much blowing of the whistle and popping of steam, a small steam engine came backing up and, with a jolt, would couple on the cars for the trip up the mountain. At this time, the baggage for the passengers going up the mountain were transferred and the passengers climbed aboard. Soon, the train, with a grinding of wheels and puffing of smoke, slowly moved up the track, which paralleled the main track for about one mile, then curved over the main line as it went into the tunnel, and started up the mountain."

As the train approached the Monteagle railroad depot, "there was great excitement looking out the window to see who was at the station, calling to friends, and trying to be the first off. There was a lot of hollering, hugging, and kissing after the train stopped. You would wait until the trunks were unloaded so you could identify yours and give the baggage checks. Your trunks would be delivered to your cottage on the trunk wagon. Then you would climb into one of the carriages to go to the front gate and get your tickets. The kids usually hopped out of the carriages and ran to get to their cottages first."

The Monteagle depot was only yards away from the Assembly front gate, down the tracks to the right. The 1910 photograph shows a large water tank across the tracks from the depot, as well as several horse-drawn hacks waiting to take passengers either to the Assembly or to the Monteagle Hotel a short distance down College Street.

For many years, Mr. Jim Long used to bring all the trunks to the Assembly. In 1980, Mrs. Joseph "Opie" Handley recalled him as being, "an elderly, black-hatted man who wore a long handlebar mustache."

Waverly-Dickson Accommodation

The Contributor 1/4/2016

During the past several years there has been considerable discussion in Nashville about the possibility of using CSX railroad lines to provide passenger service to Nashville for commuters and shoppers who live on the edges or outside the Nashville Metropolitan area.

Most Nashvillians don't know that in 1907, the NC&StL Railroad inaugurated what was called the "Waverly-Dickson Accommodation." The new service was designed to transport, in five passenger cars, about 200 residents of Waverly and other towns and villages along the line to Nashville's Union Station.

Each workday, train No. 7 arrived at Union Station at 8 a.m. or earlier. Each afternoon, train No. 8 pulled out of Union Station at 5:30 p.m. to return its commuters to their home communities. The first two stops out of Nashville were at the Round House and at St. Mary's Orphanage. This valuable service ended in 1929.

The NC&StL offered, for a number of years, a similar service for commuters and shoppers who lived along the Nashville and Chattanooga Division of the railroad. This service began by 1884 when a train left Cowan daily at 6 a.m. and arrived at Nashville's Union Station at 9:37 a.m. The reverse direction train left Union Station daily at 4 p.m. and arrived at Cowan at 7 p.m. This train stopped at Decherd, Tullahoma, Normandy, Wartrace, Bell Buckle, Christiana, Murfreesboro, Smyrna, Antioch, and Glencliff. By 1934, the local service between Cowan and Nashville had ceased, probably because of the impact of the Depression.

Dixie Flyer train leaving Wartrace, Tennessee
Collection of Ridley Wills II

Restaurants

Rotier's Restaurant

The Contributor 10/27/2021

John and Evelyn Rotier started Rotier's Restaurant in 1945 in a building on Elliston Place that earlier had been the carriage house for "Burlington," a palatial home built by William R. Elliston in 1850.

Originally called Al's Tavern, the restaurant started as a beer joint with pinball machines and cheeseburgers. One of those who frequented it was Leo Long, the veteran coach at nearby Father Ryan High School. In the summer of 1951, Leo met his friend Howard Allen at Al's Tavern soon after Allen had been fired as MBA's coach by headmaster Richard Sager. Leo told Allen that, if he came to Father Ryan, he could take his place as head football coach and Leo would coach the school's basketball team. Allen did so and coached the Ryan football team for two years before moving to Texas.

Later in the 1950s, Martin McNamara Jr. worked at Al's Tavern for two years, earning the money he needed to attend Vanderbilt. Martin fondly remembers "Lost John," Al's Tavern maintenance man for a number of years. John lived in the basement of the apartment building across the street, where he also performed maintenance, including stoking the coal furnace.

Among the many Vanderbilt students who frequented Al's Tavern was Clarence "Babe" Taylor, an SAE (Sigma Alpha Epsilon) and, in

1956, a second team all-SEC basketball player. On more than one occasion, Babe had a beer at Al's Tavern not long before going to Memorial Gymnasium for a game.

In time, Al's Tavern became a full-scale meat-and-three restaurant. John and Evelyn had three children—John Jr., Margaret, and Charlie—who worked there with their parents. When John Jr. took over, the restaurant's specialty was a cheeseburger on French bread. By 1973, John Jr. changed his restaurant's name to Rotier's. The restaurant also received a national award from *USA Today* and recognition from *Food Network Magazine*.

Before reaching its 75th anniversary in 2020, a third generation of the Rotier family was in charge. In 2021, seventy-six years of good food came to an end as GBT Realty announced that it had acquired Rotier's, a drive-through Smoothie chain, and one or two other businesses and had plans, approved by the Metro Council, to build a 27-story tower called "The Sinclair" in the triangle between West End and Elliston Place at 2416 West End Avenue. GBT's plan is to break ground in the fourth quarter of 2022.

Night view of the front of Rotier's Restaurant

Wagon Wheel Restaurant

The Contributor 3/31/2021

Wagon Wheel Restaurant was proof that good times and good places don't last forever. Almost no one alive today can remember the Wagon Wheel Restaurant, which opened in 1934 near the split of Highways 70 and 100 just outside Belle Meade.

The Wagon Wheel was advertised as having Nashville's largest dance floor, accommodating 500. On the night of its opening, Jimmy Gallagher's orchestra was featured. In July 1934, Beasley Smith and his orchestra were originating some of their programs from the ballroom of the Wagon Wheel, broadcast over radio station WLAC from 11–11:30 each evening.

The next month, Francis Craig brought his orchestra, which featured "Pee Wee" Marquette from Montgomery, Alabama, to the Wagon Wheel.

In August 1935, Ozzie Nelson and his orchestra appeared there. His vocalist was Harriet Hilliard, who married Ozzie later that year. That night, the owners had enlarged the terrace to hold the large crowd expected. On Saturday September 11, 1937, Jackie Coogan brought his orchestra to the Wagon Wheel.

Throughout the late 1930s, dance contests were also regularly held at the Wagon Wheel. They featured waltzes and swing music, sponsored by such organizations as the Knights of Columbus and the Elks Club.

The Wagon Wheel didn't make it through the Depression. By the end of 1937, its new owner, Chet Eakle, was having a hard time. In March 1938, an involuntary petition for bankruptcy was filed against him. The property was sold by the trustee to Howard M. Werthan, Leah Rose Werthan, and Mary Jane Werthan. The nightclub remained open, however, and, on the evening of May 10, 1939, Tommy Dorsey brought his orchestra to the Wagon Wheel for a return visit. In early June 1939, the nightclub closed for a few days only to reopen on

June 17 under the ownership of Jack Price Jones. A month later, after the nightclub closed at 2 a.m. on the morning of July 19, 1939, the Wagon Wheel burned to the ground. Good times and good places never last forever.

In 1934 Francis Craig and his orchestra performed at Wagon Wheel Restaurant.

Rivers

A Short History of Steamboats in Middle Tennessee

The Contributor 3/27/2019

Many Nashvillians are fascinated with steamboats and know that the first steamboat to reach Nashville was the *General Jackson*, which arrived at the Nashville Wharf on March 11, 1819. It had come from New Orleans to the Harpeth Shoals in twenty-one days and six hours. The *General Jackson* remained there for several days unloading when a rise in water allowed it to come the last twenty miles to Nashville.

By 1830, steamboating was big business in Nashville. If you have ever wondered whether steamboats ever made it to Columbia on the Duck River, the answer is yes although the perilous steamboat run to Columbia proved unprofitable. Here is my proof: Alderman St. Leger White, one of Columbia's oldest citizens, once said, "I remember when the first steamboat ever landed in Columbia. It was in 1843 and was named the *Madison*. My father was fishing near where the old bridge was located the day she arrived. He caught more fish that day than he ever did in his life. The boat had stirred up the river and frightened the fish making them easy to catch. The *Madison* and the *Lily of the West* made a number of trips from Columbia to the Tennessee River and did a fine business, carrying freight" for several months when the water was high.

The Red River was the only navigable tributary of the Cumberland that entered it from the north. In the nineteenth century, top-water or light draft steamboats and barges plied the Red River a distance of twenty-five miles up to Port Royal. The *Red River* was one of the first steamboats to reach Port Royal.

The Caney Fork is the Cumberland's largest tributary. Its mouth is on the east side of the Cumberland slightly above Carthage, which is on the Cumberland's west bank. The first steamboat to ply the Caney Fork was the *Harry Hill*. In 1832 it made an historic trip up the Caney Fork on a huge tide to Sligo Landing, fifteen land miles from Sparta. Carthage, where the *Harry Hill's* hull had been hewed at Sligo Landing, was always considered a good river town.

Celina is located at the mouth of the Obey River, one of the largest navigable tributaries of the Cumberland. Located in the heart of Tennessee's hardwood timber belt, the Obey was navigated by barges and rafts by 1840. No doubt some fearless steamboat pilot during these

Top: The steamboat *Electra* at the Nashville Wharf—the Shelby Street Bridge is in the background, ca. 1910–15.

The *Robert Rhea* steamboat navigates the Cumberland River near Carthage, Tennessee.

Tennessee State Library and Archives

days must have explored the river for some distance. However, packet owners were more interested in conquering the upper Cumberland, which had more water than the Caney Fork or the Obey. By 1840, there were twelve principal river landings on the upper Cumberland in the State of Kentucky.

Steamboating on the Caney Fork

The Contributor 11/10/2021

The Caney Fork is the largest tributary of the Cumberland River, and one of the most beautiful rivers in Tennessee. It starts as a small stream north of Pleasant Hill in Cumberland County, continues generally south to Pilot Falls where it drops from the Cumberland Plateau into "The Gulf." The river then flows in a western direction through

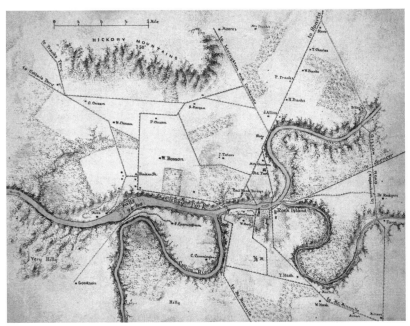

Sketch of the vicinity of the falls on Caney Fork of the Cumberland River
J. E. Weyss, April 1863, Library of Congress

"The Gulf'" before emerging from between high hills at the lower end of Big Bottom, twenty-six miles upstream from Great Falls. From the falls, it continues through a gorge for about eight miles to below the old Franks Ferry, where the valley opens up and there are many fertile farms, to empty into the Cumberland River a mile upstream from Carthage.

The first steamboat of record to ply the shallow Caney Fork was the *Harry Hill*. The timber for the boat's hull was hewed out by Sam Caplinger and William Christian at Caplinger's Mill near Carthage in 1832. The hull was floated to Nashville where machinery was installed. The boat then returned to Carthage that same year and made her historic trip up the Caney Fork. On a huge tide, she made it all the way to Sligo Landing in Dekalb County, fifteen miles by land from Sparta. In time, the *Harry Hill* became a leading packet on the Cumberland. On December 17, 1846, a second boat, under Captain A. Davis made it all the way to Oakland, also about fifteen miles from Sparta.

From 1910 to 1915 there was a gradual reduction in commercial freight on the Upper Cumberland. By 1920, improved highways and trucks began to eat the very heart out of the packet business. Even the Burnside packets, operating in the most remote section of the river felt the impact of motor vehicle competition. Between 1920 and 1930, very seldom did someone see a steamboat on the Cumberland above Nashville. A few small towboats engaged in handling crossties on the upper river. Some of them may have ventured up the lower section of the Caney Fork for that purpose.

Muscle Shoals

publication date unknown

Until Wilson Dam was constructed in 1924, Florence and Tuscumbia, Alabama, marked the head of steamboat navigation on the Tennessee River. This meant that, until railroads penetrated East

Tennessee, the citizens of Knoxville had to rely largely on homespun clothes, while Nashvillians, who gained steamboat access to New Orleans on the Cumberland, Ohio, and Mississippi rivers, beginning in the spring of 1819, had access to china, clothing, coffee, cutlery, furniture, plows, and sugar.

In the 1820s, Knoxvillians began to campaign for steamboat transportation through Muscle Shoals. To entice some intrepid steamboat captain to try to reach Knoxville from Paducah, the city offered a handsome prize for the first steamboat to tie up on the Knoxville landing. In 1827, the *Atlas*, a small side-wheeler, built in Cincinnati, won the purse by becoming the first steamboat to navigate the Tennessee from Paducah to Knoxville. After tying his boat up at Florence for several days waiting for high enough water, the *Atlas* made it through Muscle Shoals on February 15, 1828. After enjoying the hospitality of North Alabama for a few days, Captain S. D. Connor continued east headed to the perils of the Narrows. That stretch of river proved less formidable than had been anticipated. The *Atlas* passed through the Boiling Pot in fifteen minutes and came through the Suck in only nine minutes. The *Atlas* had only one warp between the Narrows and Knoxville. The slow time up the upper Tennessee River was not due to navigation difficulties but to the frequent stops for wood. As there were no woodyards on the upper Tennessee, Captain Connor had to stop every now and then for his crew to go ashore and chop wood to fuel the boat.

The *Atlas* arrived at Knoxville after dark on March 3. There the mayor and aldermen were on hand for a ceremonial welcome. The *Atlas* turned around in the mouth of the French Broad and returned safely to the Ohio, never to venture to Knoxville again.

During the 1830s, only eight small steamboats reached Knoxville from Decatur, Alabama. The first to attempt to provide regular packet service between Knoxville and Decatur was the *Knoxville*. She became a financial failure because getting through the Boiling Pot and the Suck was so difficult. In 1834, the *Reliance*, headed to Knoxville from Florence, in a day's time, only managed to get one mile upstream in the Muscle Shoals.

Before the Civil War, the lower Tennessee River was served mainly by packets of the Northern owned lines, many of which operated out of St. Louis. Packets from that city would come up the Tennessee as far as Clifton, where they would pick up railroad ties to take back to St. Louis.

During the Civil War, the Tennessee River was divided into two parts—the lower river below Florence, and the upper river between Decatur and Knoxville. This was a great advantage to the Confederates because Yankee ironclads could not reach Confederate-occupied Chattanooga and Knoxville.

In the fall of 1863, after U.S. Grant assumed command of all Union forces in the Military Division of the Mississippi, he began building gunboats above Muscle Shoals. Some steamboats managed to get as close to Chattanooga as Bridgeport, Alabama. In December 1863, after the Union victories on Missionary Ridge and Lookout Mountain, a steamboat carried my great-grandfather, Jesse Ely, a Confederate private, who had been captured at a Confederate Signal Station on Signal Mountain, from Bridgeport to prison at Rock Island, Illinois.

Steamboats prospered during the reconstruction years as there was little competition from debt-ridden railroads because long stretches of road had to be rebuilt and so much rolling stock had been destroyed during the war. Within fifteen years after the close of the Civil War, steamboat traffic on the Tennessee, particularly on the upper river, was thriving. Between 1865 and 1900, at least thirty-eight steamboats were built on the upper Tennessee. Of the fifty that operated on the upper river during this period, only an estimated half-dozen were brought

Wilson Dam and power house, Muscle Shoals, Alabama, April 11, 1926
Copyright O. T. Ericson, Library of Congress

through the Muscle Shoals, from such ports as St. Louis, Evansville, Cincinnati, and Pittsburgh.

The situation changed later in the century when railroads were more rambunctious and became great competitors. By 1900, steamboat traffic on the upper river was beginning to decline.

In Chattanooga, industrialists were clamoring for a cheap way to send their products to cities such as St. Louis and Cincinnati. They figured that, if there were river improvements, rail rates would go down and they would have two options. The pressure became intense with the result that a second Muscle Shoals canal was built. The first such effort failed forty years earlier. U.S. Army engineers began work on the second canal in 1875, and it was finally completed in 1890. The engineers successfully widened and straightened the 14.5-mile old canal and reduced the number of locks to nine. They added a short canal, with two locks, at the troublesome Elk River Shoals. The man in charge of building the canal was George W. Goethals, later the builder of the Panama Canal.

The completed canal resulted in an immediate increase in traffic on the upper river. Still there were problems. Sediment had to be continually dredged out of the canal and seasonal floods kept breaking down canal walls. Steamboats could usually make it through but modern towboats with their strings of barges were often wrecked. By the 1920s, steamboat traffic on the upper river had almost vanished.

In 1913, the Chattanooga and Tennessee River Power Company completed the Hales Bar Dam at Guild, Tennessee. Situated at the southwest end of the Narrows, it tamed the Boiling Pot and the Suck and its construction gave jobs to long out-of-work miners when the nearby Tennessee Coal, Iron and Railroad Company moved its main office to Birmingham from Tracy City in 1895.

In 1924, the U.S. Corp of Engineers completed the massive Wilson Dam between Lauderdale and Colbert Counties, Alabama, eliminating Muscle Shoals. The dam, 137 feet high, had a main lock with a lift of 94 feet. Finally, towboats with a string of barges could go from Paducah to Knoxville without a single shoal to worry about.

Roads and Streets

Natchez Trace

The Contributor 6/13/2016

The Natchez Trace was known by many names. Its south end, near Natchez, Mississippi, was an old Indian trail winding around bogs and swamps, making long detours to the best fording places across streams. The trail connected the Natchez Tribes with the Choctaw Nation in north Mississippi. Further north it intersected with a path known as the Chickasaw Trail that crossed the Tennessee River at a reasonably shallow ford (Horse Ford) and then followed high ground and the crests of ridges northeastward to the Duck River. From there, the path was an animal trail, then an Indian trail following the crests of Duck River Ridge and Backbone Ridge until it veered off and followed high ground to the "Great Salt Lick" just north of Fort Nashboro.

The reason the trail primarily used high ground was to minimize the crossing of streams. During the eighteenth century, the Natchez Trace came to be used more and more by White men. French trappers, traders, and missionaries used it. Later, the English and then the French used it. In 1763, France ceded the region to England, who claimed it until they were ousted by the Spanish in 1779.

After the American Revolution, both Spain and the United States claimed the region, with the Spanish occupying the southern part and having, as their most important outpost, Natchez.

Soon after the settlement of Nashville in 1780, Americans began using the trace with Tennesseans and Kentuckians returning to their homes on the trace, having floated their flour, cotton, tobacco, and other farm products to New Orleans on flatboats and keelboats.

In 1798, Spain surrendered Natchez and all the lands north of latitude 31 degrees north to the United States. Because Natchez was of significant diplomatic, economic, and military importance, it was important to establish an adequate means of communication between Washington and Natchez. Consequently, Congress established a postal route between Nashville and Natchez even though the Postmaster General described it as "no other than an Indian footpath very devious and narrow."

Between 1786 and 1825, the United States and the Southern Indian nations signed a number of treaties restricting citizens of the United States from settling on Indian lands, defining boundaries, and providing for Americans to travel through Indian territory.

In a treaty with the Chickasaws held at Chickasaw Bluffs in 1792, the United States gained a right-of-way through their territory for a public road to be opened from Nashville to Natchez. In 1801, after permission to improve the road had been gained from both the Chickasaws and the Choctaws, Gen. James Wilkinson, commanding the United States Army in the west, had a map drawn of the Natchez Trace. Work on the road began later that year. Whether U.S. soldiers actually cleared all the road from Duck River Ridge thirty miles south of Nashville to Grindstone Ford near Port Gibson, Mississippi, is not known.

In 1806, three years after the acquisition of Louisiana, Congress provided money to make additional improvements to the road under the direction of the Postmaster General. It was estimated that the work done by the army reduced the distance from Nashville to Natchez by one hundred miles.

Beginning in 1812, one of the most famous stops on the Trace in Tennessee was at Gordon's Ferry over the Duck River, fifty-six miles from Nashville. There, Gordon and William Colbert, who also had a ferry further down on the Tennessee River, operated a trading post. Colbert was, like Gordon, a Scotsman. He, however, had joined the Chickasaw Tribe and had been made their chief. The road from Nashville passed through Williamson and Maury counties before proceeding southwest to the northwestern corner of Alabama where it crossed the Tennessee River at Colbert's Ferry. It then proceeded in a southwestern direction through Mississippi to Natchez, nearly 600 miles from Nashville.

With land-hungry immigrants intent on settling in Mississippi, southern Arkansas, and Louisiana, the trace soon became crowded not only with immigrants, but also with adventurers and fortune seekers of all descriptions, mail carriers, and flatboatmen walking home from New Orleans. As many of these men preferred to ride rather than walk up the trace, they did so on mustangs that helped fill the horse needs of fast-growing Middle Tennessee.

Besides often hostile Indians, there were many pirates on the trace. One of the most noted desperadoes was a man named Mason, who established his gang of thieves and cut-throats in a place on the Ohio River called "The Cave in the Rock." There he had a store of sorts where he sold provisions to unsuspecting flatboatmen, whom he then robbed and killed, taking their farm products to New Orleans to sell for himself and his gang. Later on, Mason established a base on the Natchez Trace where his band of outlaws terrorized anyone

Fog surrounds a portion of a bridge on Natchez Trace Parkway.
Courtesy of National Park Service, *Tennessee Magazine*

headed north or south. Soon after Mason was killed for the reward money, the notorious John A. Murrell roamed the trace murdering and plundering innocent people between 1830 and 1840. By then, the Natchez Trace was in steep decline because of the coming of the steamboat.

The first steamboat to go from Pittsburgh to New Orleans did so in 1811. By 1819, a steamboat made its initial trip from New Orleans to Nashville. By 1824, a dozen steamboats regularly plied the rivers between Nashville and New Orleans. Nevertheless, the bulk of Mississippi River traffic was carried by keelboats, flatboats, and barges well after 1819.

Today, the Natchez Trace Parkway, a national two-lane parkway, generally follows the original Natchez Trace 444 miles between Nashville and Natchez, Mississippi.

Broadway Looking toward Union Station

The Contributor 8/10/2015

This view of Broadway looking toward downtown from about 16th Avenue North was taken early in the twentieth century. Conspicuous in the photograph are the streetcar coming out Broadway, Union Station in the distance with its bronze statue of Mercury on top of its tall tower, and Moore Memorial Presbyterian Church, dedicated March 22, 1874, at 1507-09 Broadway.

Moore Memorial was named for Dr. Thomas Verner Moore, who was pastor of Nashville's First Presbyterian Church from 1869 until his untimely death in 1871. It had been his desire to erect a church edifice in the western portion of the city and, with that object in view, he induced certain members of his church to start a mission school in West Nashville. This became Moore Memorial Presbyterian Church.

Broadway Looking toward Union Station   Collection of Ridley Wills II

In 1937, having decided to relocate the church further west to Harding Road in the Richland section, the congregation voted to change its name to Westminster Presbyterian Church. The new Colonial-style building, designed by Edwin A. Keeble and Francis B. Warfield, was dedicated in September 1939.

When this Broadway photograph was taken, handsome homes stretched all the way west from Union Station to Centennial Park on the right and Vanderbilt University on the left.

Cedar Street (1880)

The Contributor 4/11/2021

With this article is an 1880 photograph of the handsome residence built by George Washington Campbell in 1844 on Cedar Street across from the front entrance to the State Capitol. Campbell had earlier lived in a townhouse on the crown of what was then called Campbell's Hill. He sold that house and four acres of land to the State of Tennessee in 1843 for $30,000 as the site for the new State Capitol.

When the state purchased the Campbell property, it was already encompassed by a stone wall. The three-story mansion Campbell built included property that extended from Vine to High Street.

Campbell, a native of Scotland and a graduate of the College of New Jersey, moved to Nashville in 1810 when he was forty-one. He was appointed a Tennessee congressman, senator, and state supreme court justice and was a close friend and adviser to residents James Monroe and Thomas Jefferson. Campbell had also been "one of the chief pillars" of President Madison's administration and served as his Secretary of the Treasury.

Campbell, a lawyer, was an early supporter of Andrew Jackson. In 1818, he was appointed minister to Russia and moved to St. Petersburg with his wife and family. While there, three of their small children died. Shattered by grief, Campbell resigned his foreign post and returned to Nashville in 1921 with his wife and surviving baby daughter, Elizabeth "Lizinka."

Back home, Campbell bought 193 acres surrounding a hilltop site three miles from town on the Franklin Pike. The next year he purchased 22 more acres and began building his new country home. While it was under construction, the Campbells lived in their townhouse on Campbell Hill. In 1839, Campbell gave his country home,

Campbell house on Cedar Street, Nashville

Collection of Ridley Wills II

which he loved, to his daughter, Lizinka, as a wedding present. Campbell lived the last four years of his life in his mansion on Cedar Street, dying here February 17, 1848, at age seventy-nine.

Later, the Cedar Street house was occupied by Governors Andrew Johnson and Parson Brownlow. In 1868, the Catholic Church purchased the mansion and added a mansard roof and cupola. Today, the Legislative Plaza occupies the property where the Campbell house long stood.

In the 1880 photograph, look down Cedar Street toward the public square and you will see the outline of St. Mary's Catholic Church built on the northeast corner of Cedar and Summer Street in 1845–47 by Adolphus Heiman. It was the first permanent Roman Catholic Church in Tennessee. Gone by 1880 were the slave pens that were once on Cedar Street closer to the public square.

Today Cedar Street, so named because of the many cedar trees on Campbell's Hill, is Charlotte Avenue, named for Charlotte Robertson, the wife of Nashville's cofounder, James Robertson.

Church Street (1901)

The Contributor 11/9/2015

This view, taken from in front of McKendree United Methodist Church, looks west on Church Street. In the lower left corner of the photograph notice the very small section of wrought iron fence that separated the street from the church's front yard.

McKendree was a handsome, Gothic-style building with a steeple 230 feet high. The sanctuary built on the site of an earlier McKendree Methodist Church, was dedicated January 29, 1879, by Bishop Holland McTyeire, who is also remembered for securing the money from Commodore Vanderbilt to establish Vanderbilt University in 1873.

The seven-story brick building in the middle right of the photograph was the Wilcox Building on the northwest corner of Church and High Streets. This building was erected in 1895 by J. M. Wilcox, of Philadelphia, on what may have been Nashville's most expensive corner. In December that year, the Wilcox Building housed the *Confederate Veterans's Magazine*, the offices of the Tennessee Centennial Celebration, and those of the L&N Railroad. The building was considered at the time of its completion to be one of the city's most handsome and best-lit business structures. It featured a large central shaft that supplied plenty of light and air. Today, the building still stands at Sixth and Church. Streets. For parts of five decades, ending in 1984, the Wilcox Building was occupied by Harvey's Department Store.

Nashville's Church Street, 1901
Collection of Ridley Wills II

Harding Road (1947)

The Contributor 4/24/2016

The view of Harding Road accompanying this article was taken by Bob Grannis [known for his stout size as "Nashville's Largest Photographer"] in 1947. On the right is the single track of the NC&StL Railroad's main line between Nashville and Memphis.

On the left side of the highway were the Belle Meade ESSO Station, and, to its right, the Belle Meade Motel, both visible in the photograph. In the indistinct distance on the east side of Harding Road was Lawson's Service Station on the southeast corner of Harding Road and Harding Place. Directly across the street from the service station was Waters Grocery, where my mother shopped. This building, unseen in Grannis's photograph, is still standing as an automobile dealership.

The Belle Meade Motel started as a tourist camp, run in 1940 by Ann M. Bomar. In 1942, John R. Bomar Jr. was its manager. He was followed by H. B. Alexander, who lived in a home he had built in 1920 on Richland Creek where the Belle Meade Terrace Apartments are today.

In about 1946, Clyde and Ruth Stamper ran the Belle Meade Tourist Camp. They changed its name in 1947 to the Belle Meade Motel.

During the 1960s and 1970s, the 25-room motel was closed and in the hands of a receiver. In 1981, Gary Smith purchased the motel from the First American National Bank and operated it, primarily as a restaurant. His specialties were fried chicken and steak and biscuits. Also popular were bacon and eggs, turnip greens, Reelfoot Lake crappie [Gary's wife is from Lake County, Tennessee] and wild game. Today, the Belle Meade Galleria occupies the site. Gary still regrets that he lost his lease.

Harding Road, 1947
Collection of Ridley Wills II

Nashville's Public Square Served as the City's Farmers Market (1900)

The Contributor 11/17/2014

This photograph of Nashville's public square, taken in 1900 from Deaderick Street, looks north toward the intersection of North Market and Bridge streets. City Hall is partially visible on the left and the white columns of the Davidson County Courthouse are shown on the right. A line of trees separated the Courthouse from the farm wagons that filled the south half of the public square.

Fridays and Saturdays were always big days on the public square, while nothing was sold on Sundays because Blue Laws strictly controlled work, commerce, and entertainment on Sundays. Between the opening hours of 4 a.m. and daylight, the city's grocers, hotel and steamboat cooks were on the square, looking for the freshest vegetables, butter, eggs, and the plumpest hens. All night long, farmers arrived to be ready for their customers. Some farmers slept in their wagons.

A Saturday morning on the Public Square, showing the courthouse on the right and farmers' wagons on the left   Collection of Ridley Wills II

By the time future sportswriter Grantland Rice was twelve years old in 1892, he was working on Saturdays a sixteen-hour day, beginning as early as 3 a.m. when he would get up and load a wagon with produce and drive it from his father's farm on Vaughn Pike to the market on the public square, sell his produce, and return home by 5:30 or 6 p.m.

Housewives often came before breakfast but not as early as the cooks and grocers. By 7 a.m., most vendors had sold their produce and were headed home to get in a full day's work on their farms. Truck farmers from Paradise Ridge took pride in arriving at the public square first and selling first.

The farmers' market was open year-round. During the winters, a smaller number of farmers sold chickens, eggs, butter, turnips, turnip greens, spinach, and sweet potatoes.

Hillsboro Turnpike
Survives Civil War to Become a Free Pike
The Contributor 8/15/2016

Tennessee's General Assembly created the Nashville and Hillsboro Turnpike Company on February 3, 1848. The act stipulated that the capital of the company should be $100,000, to be increased, if necessary, to build a macadamized road from Nashville to the foot of the Duck River Ridge—three miles beyond Hillsboro (now Leiper's Fork) in Williamson County and in the direction of Williamsport in Maury County.

According to the act, the road should begin at the mouth of Broad Street in Nashville, today's 10th Avenue South, "and extend through the lands of John Boyd's heirs, thence so that a southwardly line will strike the lands of Benjamin Litton, thence through his lands nearly south until it strikes the lands of John Bain, Alexander B. Montgomery, Samuel Watkins, the Castlemans, John Boyd's and H. W.

Compton's tracts of land, passing through two gaps of the hills east of the Compton residence, so as to intersect the Compton Road near the Cartwrights's old place, Willoughby Williams, then crossing the Big Harpeth . . . in the general direction of Hillsboro in Williamson County."

The act further reads, "That Felix Compton, William P. Cloyd, William Edmonson and Joseph Motherell shall be commissioners to locate such road. . . . That the company is authorized to demand and receive tolls at each gate not exceeding the following rates, viz: for every 20 head of sheep or hogs 10 cents; for every twenty head of horned or meat cattle 25 cents; for every horse or mule not employed in drawing a carriage 03 cents; for every pleasure carriage drawn by two or more horses or mules 25 cents; if drawn by three or more horses or mules 35 cents, provided that every wagon, drawn by more than six horses, mules or oxen may be charged 10 cents for each horse, mule or oxen over six, unless the tire of said wagon shall be at least four inches wide."

The act further provided that the number of gates to be erected upon said road shall not exceed five and no two gates shall be nearer to each other than five miles.

In 1861, when the Civil War began, twenty miles of the Hillsboro Turnpike were complete, stretching from the city limits at today's 10th Avenue South to Perkins Lane in Williamson County.

Walter Stokes Sr., who lived on the road, wrote, "That long stretch of smooth road was ground to dust by the Confederate and Union armies, and the bridge over the Big Harpeth was destroyed."

The greatest excitement during the war came on December 15 and 16, 1864, when the right wing of Rosecrans's Federal Army swept across Hillsboro Turnpike to rout John Bell Hood's Army of Tennessee in the last great battle of the Civil War.

After the Civil War, the turnpike owners struggled to rebuild. In about 1871, a surveyor was employed to survey the unfinished eight miles of the road between Perkins Lane and the Duck River Ridge. About this time, the new bridge across the Big Harpeth had been swept away by a flood.

Hillsboro Pike, 1887, at the corner of today's Belcourt Avenue and 21st Avenue
South in Hillsboro Village   *Art Work of Nashville*

Also, the Nashville and Hillsboro Turnpike Company became
embroiled in litigation which resulted in Thomas J. O'Keefe purchasing its assets for $7,785.72 in 1883. On September 2 of that year,
O'Keefe conveyed the property to James C. Bradford, Samuel Clay-
brook, and Samuel Perkins, who incorporated under the name "Nashville and Duck River Ridge Turnpike Company." As a byproduct of
the litigation, the Nashville and Hillsboro Turnpike Company appropriated the use of the right-of-way between Hillsboro (Leiper's Fork)
and the Duck River Ridge, a distance of three miles. Consequently, the
Nashville and Duck River Ridge Turnpike Company was shortened
from twenty-eight to twenty-five miles and had its southern terminus
at Leiper's Fork, the former home of Senator Thomas Hart Benton.

One and one-half miles from Nashville, two stone pillars on
Hillsboro Pike across the street from Edgehill Avenue, marked the
south entrance to Vanderbilt. From the pillars swung an iron gate
which was locked at night and on Sundays to reserve the privacy of the
small Methodist university and keep out livestock. Identical iron gates
were at the end of Broadway and on West End Avenue at the gymnasium. A board fence enclosed the campus.

By 1899, the Hillsboro Turnpike was in such poor condition that the road commissioner ordered the gates to be lifted. When the owners refused to comply, the commissioner "recommended that the grand jury take action." Somehow a compromise was reached and in 1900, the commissioner declared Hillsboro Pike to be in "fair condition."

In February 1902, the eight miles of Hillsboro Turnpike and all the other turnpikes in Davidson County were purchased by the county. The Hillsboro Turnpike owners received a total of $10,000. Hillsboro became in 1902 a free pike to the county. The "Free the Turnpikes" movement had started in 1895.

A February 1912 article in a local newspaper reported that real estate values along Hillsboro Pike had been advancing rapidly, particularly since the widening of Hillsboro Pike to seventy feet and the completion of the Hillsboro car line.

American Baptist College
Courtesy of American Baptist College

Schools

American Baptist College

The Contributor 5/23/2016

At its annual meeting in 1913, the National Baptist Convention appointed a committee to investigate the possibility of establishing a seminary to educate its ministers. That same year, the Southern Baptist Convention appointed a similar committee. In 1914, the committees of the two conventions met and recommended that the seminary be established in Memphis. Later, the recommendation was changed to recommend a Nashville site for the seminary.

Slowed by the Great World War, the National Baptists purchased the present 53-acre site on the northside of the Cumberland River in 1921 and erected, in 1923, the first building, Griggs Hall.

It housed classrooms, a dining hall, dormitory rooms, and a library. American Baptist College (ABC), formerly the American Baptist Theological Seminary, formally opened on September 14, 1924.

In 1937, the Southern Baptist Convention agreed to equally share costs of the college with the National Baptist Convention USA. This partnership fostered a climate at the school that helped prepare students to meet the challenges of the Civil Rights movement led by Dr. Martin Luther King Jr.

In 1960, students from American Baptist College, including C. T. Vivian, Bernard Lafayette, Jim Bevel, William Barbee, and John Lewis were on the front line in the Nashville sit-in movement for justice and change. Despite being one of the poorest schools in America, it is likely that ABC produced more important civil rights leaders than did Tennessee State University and Fisk combined. On April 19, 1960, Lafayette helped lead the march to the historic confrontation with Nashville Mayor Ben West.

Since the 1960s, as before, ABC has struggled financially. In 1996, a decision was made to turn the assets of the college over to the board of trustees of the American Baptist College. To this day, the college tries to live by the Scripture which admonishes us "to do justice, to love mercy, and to walk humbly before God."

The school's mission is "to educate its students to become leaders in whatever profession of their choosing, instilling in them a passion to advance God's mission of justice, compassion, and reconciliation." Dr. Forrest E. Harris Jr. is president of American Baptist College, whose motto is "Light a Flame That Lasts Forever." One of his many challenges is to complete the restoration of Griggs Hall and extinguish its debt.

The American Baptist College is at 1800 Baptist World Center Drive, Nashville, Tennessee, 37207.

Buford College

The Contributor 4/18/2016

In 1886, Mrs. Elizabeth Burgess Buford, who taught for a year at Dr. Price's College for Young Ladies in Nashville, started her own school in Clarksville. In 1901, Mrs. Buford moved her school to Davidson County where Nashville businessman Oscar F. Noel agreed to let her use, rent-free, twenty-five acres of land in today's Oak Hill, south of Caldwell Lane and east of Outer Drive. He also agreed to pay for the cost of a school building. The only condition was that, upon his death or hers, the property would revert to Noel's heirs. Mrs. Buford accepted those terms and the building was built in "a virgin forest of giant oaks and magnolias." She then began recruiting young ladies between the ages of sixteen and twenty as students, and faculty members whom she wanted to be "cultured, Christian women, to the manor born."

One easy recruit was Mrs. Buford's sister, Miss Louise Chamberlis Burgess, who would be director of music. There were thirteen other subjects: English, Mathematics, History, Natural Science, Language, Religion, Philosophy, Domestic Science, Phonography [shorthand], Journalism, Library Training, Expression, and Art.

By 1907, Buford College had grown to the point that a new building was needed. Mr. Noel and his business partner, Frank Boensch, generously paid for the new building and extended the school's lease until 1915. The new facility enabled Mrs. Buford to increase enrollment from 65 to 120 girls. Now, in addition to two buildings, she had tennis courts, a garden, dairy, hennery, steam heat, electricity, a water plant, laundry, and bakery.

In a promotional piece mailed to parents in 1911, Mrs. Buford bragged that there had been "no death, no elopement, no casualty in [the] history of [the] college."

The good times changed after Mr. Noel died in 1914. His heirs began pressuring Mrs. Buford to return their property. Buford College's last school year on the Noel land was in 1915–16. In 1917, Eb Buford, Mrs. Buford's husband, filed a Confederate pension claim. In

Buford College   Collection of Ridley Wills II

it, he wrote that he and Mrs. Buford had been "engaged in school business in Nashville" the previous year but "have been deprived of this, and are now without means."

When the property reverted to the Noel family in the summer of 1916, Buford College moved to the old Sam Murphy place on the north side of Church Street between 20th and 21st avenues north.

In 1917 or 1918, the school moved again, this time to "Edgewood," the former home of Johnson and Annie Mary Bransford, who, in 1914, had subdivided their property on what is now North 12th Street, and moved to "Deerfield" in Belle Meade.

Eb Buford died in 1919, leaving Elizabeth to handle the school's business affairs and everything else. Her health failed precipitously in January 1920 and she died on February 12 of that year at age seventy-one. Her school had been a good one.

Fisk University's History

The Contributor 7/17/2019

In 1880, W. W. Clayton wrote in his *History of Davidson County,* "Fisk University is the leading institution in the great Southwest for the education of colored people."

Fisk University was born in October 1865 as a school for Black students in several abandoned hospital buildings known as the Railroad Hospital. Located near the Nashville and Chattanooga Railroad Depot [where the north Gulch is in 2022], the school was sponsored by the American Missionary Association, and the Western Freedmen's Aid Commission.

Fisk School and later Fisk University were named in honor of General Clinton B. Fisk. Following the Civil War, General Fisk, "an avowed abolitionist who neither drank nor swore," was named assistant commissioner of the Freedmen's Bureau for Kentucky and Tennessee. He is considered the founder of Fisk University, which was chartered on August 22, 1867.

By 1870, the university buildings and location were inadequate for a school of such promise and popularity. George L. White, music teacher at Fisk since its early days, suggested that he take his small company of student singers to the North to sing popular songs and raise money to purchase a more appropriate site for the school. The singers went and raised $20,000 by May 1872.

In the spring of 1874, White took his singers, who were known as the "Fisk Jubilee Singers," to England, where they were received enthusiastically and where they performed before her Majesty the Queen. In a year abroad, during which time they toured six countries, the Jubilee Singers raised $150,000.

Fisk had sufficient funds in 1892 to build a chapel, a superb example of High Victorian Picturesque architecture. The Fisk Memorial Chapel features a Romanesque arched and columned front entrance, flanked by twin stone and stucco towers and a tall bell tower pierced by Gothic stone windows.

The most imposing of the twentieth-century buildings on the Fisk campus is the Administration Building, and Erastus Milo Cravath Library, built in 1929 and named for the first president of the university.

Fisk University's Jubilee Hall   Collection of Ridley Wills II

In 1930, Fisk became the first African American institution to gain accreditation by the Southern Association of Colleges and Schools.

Twenty-three years later, Phi Beta Kappa, the nation's oldest and most widely known academic honor society, granted Fisk a charter to establish the first chapter of the Phi Beta Kappa Society on a predominantly Black campus.

Fisk struggled financially during the twentieth century. Integration brought enormous benefits to the nation, but was a mixed blessing to Fisk as outstanding African American high school seniors, who, in the segregation era, would have chosen to go to Fisk or one of the other highly rated African American schools, could then go to Princeton, Yale, Harvard, and other outstanding historically White universities.

Fisk remains a predominantly African American institution with a strong liberal arts and sciences emphasis and approximately 800 students.

Tennessee's Highlander Folk School: Incubator for the Civil Rights Movement

The Contributor 7/21/2014

The school is historic, and its founders—social justice pioneers in their own right—are rightly revered as champions of civil rights. Highlander's cofounder, Myles Horton, was born in 1905 in Savannah, Tennessee. While attending college, he spent two summers organizing Vacation Bible Schools on the Cumberland Plateau.

The Rev. Abram Nightingale, a free-thinking Congregational minister from Crossville, Tennessee, influenced him to begin an adult education program at a small church fifteen miles southeast of Crossville near Ozone, Tennessee.

At Nightingale's suggestion, Horton went to New York's Union Theological Seminary in 1929. A year later, he transferred to the University of Chicago before studying folk schools in Denmark.

Horton then returned to America where he and Don West, a Vanderbilt Divinity School graduate, started their own school. Horton and West met Dr. Lilian Johnson, who operated a small agricultural co-op at Summerfield, Tennessee, near Monteagle. Johnson, ready to retire, was impressed with the young men and lent them her property for one year as an experiment. When Johnson gave Horton and West her property in 1932, they named it the Highlander Folk School. There, they began holding workshops, dispensing information on agricultural problems, discussing religion, and criticizing Southern factory and mine owners for paying rock-bottom wages.

In 1933, when West left Highlander, James Dombrowski—an Emory University graduate, Methodist minister, and socialist—and Elizabeth Hawes, another college-educated socialist, were employed by Horton.

In 1935, twenty-five-year-old Zilphia Mae Johnson joined Highlander. Five months later, she married Myles. A College of the Ozarks graduate, Zilphia, who was proficient with many musical instruments, produced at least ten books of protest songs at Highlander.

By 1936, Highlander was openly flouting Tennessee's segregation laws. Funded primarily by "drawing room radicals," as some critics dubbed them, Highlander unquestionably was helping the community. Its library, the only one in Grundy County, was open to everyone.

During the 1930s, Highlander trained labor union leaders, and helped the Congress of Industrial Organizations unite Southern and Northern mill workers into a powerful national union, the Textile Workers Organizing Committee.

In 1938, the Dies Commission, established by Congress to investigate "un-American activities," and the FBI investigated Highlander, but found nothing "of a seditious nature."

In 1939, John Burns, a *Tennessean* reporter, posing as a schoolteacher, visited Highlander. That October, the *Tennessean* published his conclusions. Burns claimed Highlander was spreading communist doctrine and that its leadership included people who "have either been charged with being communists or who have been linked definitely with Moscow." Horton denied the allegations.

In 1940 and 1941, First Lady Eleanor Roosevelt donated $100 to Highlander. In a letter to Horton, she said that, because of the attacks on Highlander, she had the school carefully checked, and concluded that critics "are not opposed to you because of any communist activities, but because they are opposed to labor organizations and, therefore, labor education. This seems to me a most unwise and shortsighted attitude. Therefore, I am continuing my support."

During World War II, Highlander conducted summer sessions for union members, ran a children's camp, held voter registration and leadership classes, and an integrated workshop for automobile workers. After the war, Highlander began conducting integrated workshops to teach Southerners how to integrate peacefully.

In 1955, Rosa Parks, a young Black woman from Montgomery, Alabama, attended a Highlander workshop, where she was treated respectfully. Before leaving, Horton told Rosa and her classmates to "return to your homes and try to make a difference." Rosa replied, "I come from the 'Cradle of the Confederacy,' and the white people wouldn't let black people do anything."

Back home in Montgomery, Rosa wrote: "The discrimination got worse and worse to bear after having, for the first time in my life, been free at Highlander."

At Highlander, Rosa met Septima Clark, a Black civil rights leader, who for nearly forty years taught school in South Carolina. When she was fired without cause, Horton hired her to direct integration workshops. On December 1, 1955, Parks sat in the "white only" section of a city bus. Her refusal to move to the "colored" section set off the historic Montgomery bus boycott.

Myles's forty-six-year-old wife, Zilphia, died in 1956 in Vanderbilt Hospital of uremic poisoning as a result of accidentally drinking carbon tetrachloride [typewriter cleaning fluid she mistook for water]. Distraught, Myles sent their children, Thorsten and Charis, to live with his sister in Murfreesboro, and, to forget his misery, immersed himself into his fight against the entrenched power structure.

When First Lady Eleanor Roosevelt visited Highlander in 1958, an integrated crowd heard her speak on the need for the South to

Highlander Folk School 25th Anniversary Session and Meeting (left
to right): Ralph Helstein, Myles Horton, Rosa Parks, unidentified man,
Septima Poinsette Clark, unidentified man, unidentified man, Charles
Gomillion, and Bernice Robinson
Photo by John Malone, *Nashville Banner* archives

guarantee equal voting rights for all citizens. In 1959, Nashville song-
writers Guy Carawan and Candie Anderson introduced Highlander
students to songs collected from union members and South Carolina
sea islanders. The melodies included "We Shall Overcome," a song
adapted from Charles Tinsley's gospel song "I'll Overcome Some Day,"
and a nineteenth-century spiritual.

In 1960, Carawan and Anderson taught student demonstrators
at Nashville's Capitol Hill Baptist Church protest songs, including
"We Shall Overcome," which became the anthem of the civil rights
movement.

In 1959, when the Tennessee State Legislature voted to investigate Highlander, Horton, feeling that Highlander's interracial pol-
icies were the problem, invited the legislators to visit and examine
his records. The *Chattanooga Times* considered the investigation a
witch hunt, while the *Chattanooga Free Press* praised the probe. At

Myles Horton, founder of Highlander Folk School, visits with First Lady Eleanor Roosevelt in 1938.

Photo by Bill Goodman, *Nashville Banner* archives; Nashville Public Library

the February 1959 hearing, local leaders testified that Highlander had a bad reputation, and that there was communist activity there. Carrington Scruggs testified that Horton was "mean as the devil, discouraged children from attending church, didn't ask ministers to say grace, that Zilphia used to dress like a Russian peasant, and that he had seen Russian-speaking students singing 'The Red Flag.'"

In 1959, state agents raided Highlander. At Horton's modest home, they found a small quantity of liquor. In his absence, they arrested Septima Clark, a teetotaler, for "possessing whiskey," even though the whiskey was neither at the school nor at her home. Others accused the Highlander staff of displaying the Russian flag, and carrying Young Communist League membership cards. The county registrar testified that Highlander's charter was not recorded in Grundy County and that school property had been deeded to Horton. The Highlander board had, in 1957, approved giving Horton his home and seventy acres in appreciation for his dedicated service.

University of the South professors Drs. Ben Cameron and Scott Bate testified for Highlander. One of them called Highlander "an inspiring example of democracy at work."

At the 1959 trial, the state charged the school, represented by Nashville attorneys Cecil Branstetter and Jordon Stokes III, with illegally selling alcohol and fostering other "immoral, lewd and unchaste practices."

The defense presented seven Sewanee professors, who attested to the character and quality of Highlander's staff and program. Horton testified that Highlander sold no alcohol but did maintain a kitty to which any adult who wanted beer contributed. Horton also admitted purchasing items for African American students because Monteagle stores refused to serve them.

The jury found Highlander guilty of peddling liquor without a license, and violating Tennessee's segregation law. When the sheriff padlocked the buildings, Horton said, "You can padlock a building but you cannot padlock an idea." After fruitless appeals, the State auctioned Highlander's 24 building and 175 acres for $43,500. Meanwhile, Horton received a charter for a new school in Knoxville—The Highlander Research and Education Center [HREC]. Now located in New Market, Tennessee, the HREC continues to pursue Highlander's original purpose of educating rural and industrial leaders.

In February 2015, fifteen years after Myles Horton's death, *National Geographic* published an article by Charles Cobb Jr., an African American author and journalist, in which he named Highlander one of seven sites most crucial to the civil rights cause.

The University of the South and Beersheba Springs

The Contributor 12/23/2020

The University of the South's early history is inextricably interwoven with that of Beersheba. The famous pre-Civil War watering hole was the scene of two meetings of the University of the South Board of Trustees. Col. John Armfield, of Beersheba, gave the first two Sewanee chancellors—Bishops James Harvey Otey of Tennessee and Leonidas Polk of Louisiana—summer homes in Beersheba. The charter of the university was granted by the State of Tennessee in January 1858. In October 1860, plans were laid in Beersheba for the laying of the cornerstone at Sewanee.

A summer resident of Beersheba, Judge Oliver J. Morgan, of Carroll Parrish, Louisiana, made the final gift needed to complete the university endowment. In appreciation for his support, Morgan's Steep on the west brow in Sewanee is named for him. Along the same brow are Otey's Prospect, Polk's Lookout, and Armfield's Bluff.

For many years, the altar that had been in Polk's Beersheba cottage was housed at different spots in Beersheba, including the Howell Cottage and the Northern Store. It finally found a permanent home in All Saints Chapel in Sewanee.

The Howell Cottage, which John Armfield earlier gave to Bishop Leonidas Polk
Beersheba Springs: A History

Ward-Belmont's Beginnings

The Contributor 9/1/2021

On September 25, 1913, Ward-Belmont opened on the 49th year of Ward Seminary and the 24th year of Belmont College. The school's president was John D. Blanton. Jennie Taylor Masson, the Ward-Belmont registrar, put an advertisement in a Monteagle Sunday

School bulletin about its summer schools. She gave a rather complete description of the school and its faculty.

In the school's academic department, there were twenty teachers, graduates, or postgraduates of Toronto University, Vassar, Wellesley, Bryn Mawr, Smith, Goucher, Chicago University, Vanderbilt, Michigan, and Columbia—a most impressive list.

Ward-Belmont was, according to its registrar, "the most complete, modern and thoroughly equipped boarding school for girls and young women in the South, and equal to the best in America."

The School of Music, the most expensively maintained in any such school in the country, had, in 1913, seventeen teachers of piano. The curriculum included voice, violin, other stringed instruments, and pipe organ.

Ward-Belmont also offered Schools of Expression, Domestic Science and Home Economy, and Art, which provided the best training in painting, drawing, and designing. In 1913, Ward-Belmont featured a superb gymnasium and swimming pool with gymnastics a specialty and a course in physical education. All rooms for boarding students

Ward-Belmont students on the front steps of Pembroke Hall
Belmont University website

were "outside rooms, commodious and attractive." Classes were small with one resident teacher for every ten resident students.

John D. Blanton, president of Ward-Belmont, had come to Nashville in 1892 as a teacher and vice-president of Ward's Seminary. His influence was strongly felt in the civic, religious, educational and fraternal life of the city. In 1928, he was named Nashville's most outstanding citizen. Dr. Blanton served as president of the Tennessee College Association, and vice-president of the Southern Association of Colleges and Secondary Schools. A devoted member of First Presbyterian Church, he died in October of 1933 at age seventy-four of pneumonia, which developed during an asthma attack.

Tennessee's state tree is the tulip poplar, since 1947, and the one at right stands in Thumping Dick Hollow in Franklin County, within the domain of the University of the South.

Courtesy of Steve Alvarez, Sewanee, Tennessee

Trees

A History of Middle Tennessee Trees

The Contributor 4/24/2019

During the Federal occupation of Nashville from February 25, 1862, until the end of the Civil War in 1865, there were thousands of Federal soldiers stationed in Nashville who were living in tents, many on the west side of town and between Edgefield and the Cumberland River on the east side. These soldiers cut down thousands of trees and disassembled nearly all the fence rails in the county to warm themselves by camp fires. Other trees and rail fences were harvested to fuel the Federal steamboats that brought soldiers and supplies to the occupied city. The Elliston Plantation west of town was said to have only two trees still standing at the end of the war. One was in the middle of today's Louise Avenue just north of Elliston Place. County plantations were also devastated. An example was "Rosemont," the home of Mary McGavock Southall on the Murfreesboro Turnpike at Mill Creek. Mary, whose husband was deceased, left her plantation soon after Federal forces occupied her land early in 1862. In poor health, she and her son, Randal, moved to "Belle Meade," the home of her sister Elizabeth McGavock Harding where Mary was bedridden with rheumatism.

On June 17, 1862, Mrs. Southall roused herself enough to ride in a carriage with Elizabeth to Rosemont. They found that the occupying Federal soldiers had recently left, and the house was a wreck. Outside, fruit trees, shrubbery, and some hardwood trees had been cut down and left to rot in the front yard. Wartime photographs from 1865 show Nashville to be almost entirely without trees, a loss that took years to remedy.

Late in the nineteenth century, there were three great areas of timber in the United States. One was the evergreen forests on the West Coast. The second was the extensive yellow pine and cypress forests of the Gulf Coast. The third was the great hardwood forests that ranged from the eastern slopes of the Appalachian Mountains to Central Arkansas and from the Ohio River to south of the Tennessee Valley.

Nashville was located at the center of this hardwood area, and for more than twenty-five years, was the leading hardwood lumber–producing center in the country. Before railroads penetrated the Upper Cumberland Plateau, logs were cut down by farmers in rural areas including Overton County, often "snaked down" winter hill-sides by mules to the closest good-sized creek. On a rise or by dyna-miting dammed-up streams, the logs painfully floated to the Caney Fork, Otey, or the South Fork of the Cumberland to eventually reach the Cumberland where they were assembled into rafts and floated to Nashville where they lined the east bank of the Cumberland River for several miles.

In 1967, when my wife and I moved to Warner Pace, a neighbor was eighty-seven-year-old Thomas E. Webb Jr. He told me that when he was a boy he walked on rafts all the way from where the railroad bridge at Shelby Park is today to town.

Cordell Hull made his first trip to Nashville as an oarsman on his father's raft. Most rafters on the upper Cumberland would go to a tavern when they reached Nashville and spend most of their money on whiskey before returning home, once again broke, on the Tennessee Central. Cordell went to a bookstore and bought his first book.

By 1908, Nashville boasted thirteen sawmill plants, with a total output of lumber exceeding eighty million feet per annum. In addition to the saw mills, Nashville had a veneer factory, a big hardwood floor-ing plant, three furniture factories, two big trunk factories, two spoke and handle plants, and numerous other wood-working establishments. It was not long, however, before Middle Tennessee's original growth of hardwood trees was virtually destroyed. Today a small remnant of original growth hardwoods are in the newly-opened section of Percy Warner Park between State Highway 100 and U.S. Highway 70.

One day in 1925, an automobile ran into the large hardwood tree standing in the middle of Louise Avenue between my grandfather Wills's house at 217 Louise Avenue [now Jimmy Kelly's Restaurant] and Elliston Place. This was said to be one of the two trees on the Elliston Plantation that survived the Civil War. There was a demand to tear the tree down as a safety hazard, but a small core of preservationists, including Chancellor James Kirkland of Vanderbilt, managed to save the tree until the 1940s. About this time, historian Stanley Horn was planting trees on his lawn on Bowling Avenue. Before he died, Mr. Horn had planted in his yard every hardwood tree that was indigenous to Middle Tennessee.

My father, Jesse Wills, also loved trees and planted unusual ones, including a fringe tree and a Japanese dogwood, in his yard at 1201 Belle Meade Boulevard. One of my favorites there was a cypress tree, now large, that he transplanted from the Tennessee River bottoms west of Nashville.

When I was growing up at my parents' home, "Meade Haven," in the 1940s, there were two lines of hackberries paralleling Belle Meade Boulevard on the western edge of the 70-acre field that separated Belle Meade Boulevard from Chickering Road. I remember people riding horses, some rented from the stable at the Percy Warner Golf Course, between the lines of hackberries. One story is that Union cavalrymen inadvertently brought hackberries to Middle Tennessee in the digestive systems of the thousands of mules that accompanied their armies.

I love trees, particularly Sugar Maples, and enjoy seeing them leaf out every spring. When I lived at Meeting of the Waters in Williamson County, we had an aged Catawba tree in our front yard. In 1990 I got the bright idea to pull off the rope-thick poison ivy vine that grew almost to its top. Helping me was Andy Dailey, a Vanderbilt student who lived there while our son, Ridley III, was restoring the house. Although I never caught poison ivy before or since, I did at that time. So did Andy.

A few years ago, my brother, Matt, who has a special love for Southern Sugar Maples, sent me one from a tree nursery. It is growing in my front yard of our cottage in the Monteagle Sunday School Assembly. Matt has growing in his yard in Colorado Springs one or more Southern Sugar Maples, two Northern Sugar Maples, seventeen Western Sugar Maples, five Vine Maples, a John Pair Caddo Sugar Maple, two Red Maples, including one more than fifty feet tall, a Rocky Mountain Maple, a low-growing Japanese Maple, and an Amun Maple from Siberia.

I'm particularly appreciative of the Nashville Tree Foundation founded in 1986 by the late Betty Brown. It does great work in planting trees, educating the public on trees, identifying the oldest and largest trees in Davidson County, and designating arboretums.

At "Glen Leven," the antebellum home of the Land Trust for Tennessee on Franklin Road, there are an incredible number of the Tree Foundation's Big Tree Contest winners, including a Black Cherry, a Southern Magnolia, and a trifoliate Orange tree that I nominated in 2013. Annually, it produces sour oranges the size of lemons.

Everyone who loves trees should stroll down the tree trail along the Cumberland River downtown established several years ago by the Nashville Tree Foundation in memory of Betty Brown.

Before closing, I would like to recognize Hiroshi Sato, the former Japanese Consulate General in Nashville. In 2012, he began planting Japanese Cherries, particularly along Hillsboro Road. They have been beautiful this spring.

Cherry tree blossoms

Waterworks

Nashville's First Water System

The Contributor 1/5/2022

The site of the present City of Nashville was chosen by the city's cofounder, James Robertson. He chose land on the southern bank of the Cumberland River because of the availability of pure water in a spring at the foot of today's Church Street. There, the first settlers built Fort Nashboro which either enclosed the spring or was within sixteen and one-half yards from it. Consequently, when Indians surrounded the fort and it was unsafe to go outside, there was plenty of water to meet the settlers' needs, either inside the fort or no more than three rods away.

Nashville's first attempt to establish a public water supply was a failure. In 1823, the city negotiated a contract with Samuel Stacker to build a pump at his saw and grist mill at what was called Spout Spring. Water mains of bored black locust and cedar logs were to be laid to the City's reservoir, which the City had already erected at the rear of the Masonic Lodge on Spring Street between Cherry and Sumner streets. Another wooden pipe water line was to be laid from the reservoir to the public square. A section of this pipe was unearthed, I suspect in 1945, by Nashville Gas Company workers who were putting in new lines on Fourth Avenue North.

Stacker worked for two years trying to build the water system. He finally succeeded in bringing water to the reservoir on an experimental basis. He had underestimated the cost of excavating rock for the ditches. The City rescinded his contract and purchased the unfinished works for $2,500.

The firm of Avery and Ward began where Stacker left off and finished his project August 19, 1826. On that day, when the plant was placed in operation, the city celebrated heralding the new water system a great success. In truth, Avery and Ward had only limited success. They were able to pipe enough water to the public square to fill the cisterns there, which were used to supply water for fire engine horses. The pumping station burned down March 3, 1830, after three and one-half years of limited service.

So, once again, Nashville was without a water system and reliant on Spout Spring. There, a deliveryman would furnish spring water in two 25-gallon barrels for 25 cents.

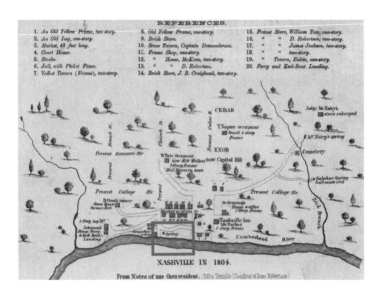

Nashville's Second Waterworks System

The Contributor 1/19/2022

Albert Stein, an experienced German engineer, was commissioned by the City of Nashville in about 1832 to build a new waterworks system. To finance the construction, the City issued its first bond issue for $50,000. The bonds were sold in Philadelphia.

Stein erected Nashville's second waterworks system on the grounds of what in 1873 became the Tennessee School for the Blind on Filmore Avenue in South Nashville. The pumping station was located on

the lower bluff close to the river where Tennessee Central Railroad tracks were built in 1902. The reservoir was immediately north of the School for the Blind where General Hospital would be built in 1890. Cast iron water mains were installed to bring the water to the city. When the system was completed October 31, 1833, the city celebrated with a grand parade, speeches, and booming cannon.

Albert Stein

The plant functioned satisfactorily for many years. Its chief problem was that muddy water from the river could not always be settled out in the reservoir. To solve this, plant superintendent James Wyatt devised an ingenious system of using naturally filtered water from the river. In about 1878, he installed a cast-iron cage that was 152 feet long, 10 feet wide, and 6 feet high, in the natural gravel beds on the Upper Island (Nashville Island) that was adjacent to the present pumping station on Omohundro Drive. River water seeped or percolated through the natural beds of gravel and sand into the collecting cage and was purified in the process. He also had workers install approximately 12,000 feet of 36-inch iron pipe along the river bank to the pumping station.

Wyatt's system of natural filtration seems to have worked very well in supplying clear water to the city for about twenty years. There were occasions, however, when the river was at its lowest levels, that it was necessary to take unfiltered water directly from the river. To extend the life of the system, the city made extensive repairs to the boilers and pumping machinery in the early 1880s.

Wilbur F. Foster partial map of Nashville, 1877, showing reservoir and pumping station

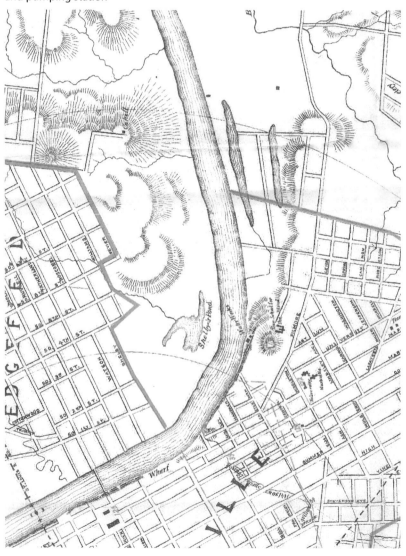

Nashville's Third Waterworks System

The Contributor 2/2/2022

In 1888, Nashville's city fathers decided to locate a new pumping station at the Upper Island, adjacent to the natural filtering system. The new plant had three 10-million-gallon pumps, and eight steam boilers, six of which had 110-horsepower and two had 400-horsepower. A new 20-million-gallon pump was ordered for delivery in 1908.

A 36-inch main led from the pumping station four miles to a new reservoir on Kirkpatrick's Hill and then to Eighth and Broad. It crossed Brown's Creek on a stone, arched bridge constructed by Foster and Creighton. In 1892, a circular stone intake was built in the Cumberland above the upper island because the water from the old filtering galleries was insufficient due to clogging of the collector pipes with mud and silt.

The system also included 110 miles of water mains. The new reservoir on Kirkpatrick's Hill beside the Franklin Pike was the former site of Fort Casino. J. A. Jowett, the city engineer, prepared the specifications and plans for the new reservoir. Whitsett & Adams submitted the lowest bid and was given the contract. Work began on August 24, 1887, and was completed August 24, 1889. The total cost was $64,525.21. Rock for the reservoir walls had been quarried from the nearby hill later called Rose Park.

The reservoir was elliptical in shape, with a major axis of 603 feet and a minor axis of 463.4 feet in the interior. The ashlar masonry wall is 22.9 feet wide at the bottom and 8 feet wide at the top. The outside wall is 33 feet high. A cross wall cuts the reservoir in half. Each compartment has a capacity of 25.5 million gallons. A gate house was built on top to hold the valves and a shelter for the custodian was erected. There was also a nine-foot-wide walkway with side walls that circled the reservoir. Before the reservoir was closed to visitors in 1917, boys raced their bicycles on the oval walkway.

Water from the pumping station entered the reservoir in the west basin. The water that came from this intake was unfiltered. It remained in the west basin until the mud settled out of it. Then, the clear water at the top flowed through a weir (channel) in the stone wall to the east basin. From there the water flowed to the distribution system. Each year, this plan was reversed so the mud at the bottom could be removed by city prisoners.

The old pumping station and reservoir at General Hospital remained available for emergency use until April 1891.

On June 26, 1908, chemical treatment of the water was begun. One twentieth of a grain of hypochlorite of lime per gallon of water was added as an oxidizing agent. This treatment was recommended by Dr. William Litterer, professor of bacteriology at Vanderbilt University, and director of the Litterer Laboratory in South Nashville. Tests made by him after this treatment of the water showed that typhoid and B-Coli germs were completely eliminated. This treatment of the water, along with sulphate of alumina, was continued until 1920, when liquid chlorine replaced hydrochlorite of lime. Liquid chlorine was used until a modern filtering plant was completed in 1930.

In the background, wearing a straw hat with hands on his hips, waterworks superintendent George Reyer oversees construction of a brick filter gallery in 1897. *Building of Nashville*

On Second Avenue South in Nashville, the former Litterer Laboratory of Bacteriology building was placed on the National Register of Historic Places in 1978.

Unfortunately, the reservoir on Kirkpatrick's Hill rested on poor bedrock on the southeast quadrant. The rock there consisted of thin ledges of limestone with thin strata of clay between them. The wide reservoir wall spread the load sufficiently to support the structure. What the designer didn't take into account were the effect of leaks. For some time in the fall of 1912 a considerable stream of water was running down the gutter on Eighth Avenue South. Major W. F. Foster, formerly city engineer, was asked to investigate the situation. He found that the stone on the southeast side of the reservoir had badly weathered, causing the leaks. Major Foster had opposed putting the reservoir on Kirkpatrick's Hill, and had supported putting it on Todd's Knob in Donelson. His suggestion was declined because it was thought that Todd's Knob was too far from town. The major predicted that the reservoir wall would fail. His prediction came true on Tuesday, November 5, 1912, when at 12:10 a.m., a section of the southeast quadrant of the reservoir broke, allowing 25 million gallons of water to pour out in a southeast direction across Eighth Avenue South toward the fairgrounds. Many houses were washed off their foundations and much property damage was done, but no one was drowned. This was miraculous because the reservoir was full and most people were in bed. The consensus was that water seepage dissolved the clay between the limestone ledges causing the stone to settle until the wall broke.

The gaping hole was filled with concrete and the walls were rebuilt using the same stone as in the original wall. The work was done by Gould Contracting Company at a cost of $70,000. In 1921, the entire interior of the reservoir was relined with granite and waterproofed. The Water Department took levels each year to detect any further settlement and, as of 1969, no leaks had been found. The reservoir still remains functional today.

Devil's Elbow during the 1951 storm— Located in what is now Joelton, the stretch of highway can be one of the most treacherous in Davidson County during icy winter weather; a rock bluff is on one side, a ravine on the other.

Photograph by W. C. Midgett, National Weather Service

Weather

The Blizzard of 1951

The Contributor 9/25/2019

On Sunday afternoon, January 28, 1951, Nashville was hit by a storm coming from the west. It left on Monday morning a coating of ice that was a taste of what was to come.

Hugh Walker, of the *Tennessean*, had more than a foot of ice and snow piled against his garage door on Monday. He poured hot water on the pile which only caused it to freeze solid. After seeing three cars stuck across the street, Hugh began walking from his home in Green Hills to his office downtown. He realized that he was walking through a silent world with no cars and no busses. Silent that is until a limb encrusted with a heavy coating of ice came crashing down on the pavement. Hugh finally made it to the Women's Club on Hillsboro beside Golf Club Lane, he went inside and called the *Tennessean*. Ed Freeman answered the phone. He told Walker, "Yes, we will publish today." Hugh resumed walking with three and one-half miles to go. Before he got very far, he saw for the first time a car. It was a little red Nash, with a new set of chains. A. J. Baird, of Baird Ward, was behind the wheel. Baird stopped and gave Hugh a ride to the *Tennessean's* front door. Walker was extremely grateful. This account was taken from the article "1951 and the Winter Wonderland" by Hugh Walker that appeared in the *Tennessean* on Sunday, February 3, 1974.

On Tuesday morning, the ice was one inch thick and the sky was "sunless." That first day there was almost no traffic. The heavy coat of ice beneath the snow was slick as glass. When graders scooped up the snow and ice on major streets, they literally buried cars parked along the side of the street. Some owners didn't dig their cars out for three or four days. Hundreds of travelers were stuck in Nashville as trains and busses quit running. Walking was dangerous as there were live wires hissing and smoking on the snow. Transformers occasionally exploded erupting in flashes of green fire.

On Wednesday night, howling winds dropped trees and limbs everywhere, temperatures plummeted, and hard sleet rattled window panes. Lights went out for 80,000 people and the heat went out over town. Later that night, the sleet changed to snow.

Nashvillians, after shivering through the night, arose on Thursday to find the city silent and the temperature at one degree below zero. Bus service was suspended and trains were eighteen hours late. The bus terminal and Union Station were packed with stranded, unhappy people.

The next morning, Friday, the weather was worse. The *Tennessean* reported that morning, February 2, that "Nashville lay like a stricken giant yesterday and last night, pinned down by a half foot layer of solid ice and four inches of snow. The temperature stood at a record-breaking thirteen degrees below zero. On that bitter day, the Red Cross declared an emergency and began evacuating people from heatless homes. The cold weather continued until February 9 when the city received another coating of ice.

The weather moderated on Sunday, February 4, and on Monday morning there were traffic jams all over town and not many policemen could be found. In addition to the slush, there were abandoned or stalled cars and trucks in the middle of the streets.

When the temperature got above freezing, broken pipes began spewing water in homes and businesses everywhere. Power linemen from N.E.S., plumbers, and electricians worked around the clock to restore electric power lines, replace broken pipes, and put homes back in order.

Every Nashvillian who lived through the Blizzard of 1951 recalled it vividly for the rest of their lives.

World War I
(The Great World War)

Camp Andrew Jackson

The Contributor 1/11/2016

After war with Germany broke out in 1917, it was learned that a National Guard camp would be built in the Nashville area. A committee of the city's prestigious Commercial Club recommended a campsite at the end of the Belle Meade Streetcar Line at what would later be the entrance to Percy Warner Park. The committee then persuaded Luke Lea, the land's owner, to lease the property to the government, which he did. Approval of the site was then obtained from Gen. Leonard Wood, mobilization director for the Southeastern United States.

Quickly, steps were taken to design streets, bring in utilities, and build wood floors for tents. The County Court approved construction of a road on either side of the streetcar line from Harding Road to the site. To provide increased water pressure for the camp and for his future residential development, Lea built a 50,000-gallon reservoir high on the nearest hill. Col. Harry Berry, of Hendersonville, Tennessee, oversaw all of this work as he was commander of the camp, which was named for Gen. Andrew Jackson.

Camp Andrew Jackson—the National Guard site built at the end of Belle Meade's streetcar line, what later would be the entrance to Percy Warner Park
Collection of Ridley Wills II

The first contingent of the 1,350-man First Tennessee Infantry Division arrived at the Harding railroad siding on April 27, 1917. Almost immediately the camp became the scene of intensive training that lasted through the summer.

On September 6, it was announced that the entire First Tennessee Infantry Division would leave Nashville by noon on September. 7. That day, four trains carried the First Tennessee and its equipment to Camp Sevier near Greenville, South Carolina. There, the First Tennessee became the 115th Field Artillery.

Back in Nashville, Camp Andrew Jackson closed. The only reminder today of Camp Andrew Jackson's existence is the granite monument on the left side of the road through Percy Warner Park, about 300 yards from the entrance gates at the end of Belle Meade Boulevard. A bronze plaque on the monument is inscribed: "To the Men of the First Tennessee Infantry Who Sleep in Honored Glory."

Old Hickory Powder Plant:
Once an Economic Force in Nashville

The Contributor 11/14/2016

The E. I. DuPont Company in 1918 built and operated an $87,000,000 powder plant for the United States Government to make smokeless powder for the Allied armies in World War I. The plant, located in Hadley's Bend, was so important to Nashville that picture postcards printed in 1918 included the caption, "Powder City of the World."

At the time of the Armistice, November 11, 1918, the plant, 75 percent complete, was producing 750,000 pounds of powder every twenty-four hours. The DuPont Company also built houses in 1917 and 1918 for its managers and thousands of workers.

1918 view of the E. I. DuPont Company's gunpowder plant, in what later became the city of Old Hickory

The area became the City of Old Hickory. However, not a single pound of powder was ever shipped to Europe. Instead, the powder was stored in barns and bins across the countryside. With the war over, the plant was shut down, Old Hickory's population plummeted from 35,000 to 500 and the War Department put up 5,600 acres for sale.

The Nashville Industrial Corporation bought the plant, then in 1923 sold it to DuPont to manufacture rayon. In the late 1940s, DuPont sold street after street of company houses in Old Hickory. Then, in the 1960s, DuPont demolished the eight giant smokestacks. Although the company no longer makes rayon, the DuPont plant still operates today as an important economic force in Old Hickory.

Hysteria Concerning German-Americans in Nashville during World War I

publication date unknown

When the First World War broke out, many Nashvillians became very suspicious of the German-Americans who were living in the city, primarily in Germantown. Col. Luke Lea, publisher of the rabidly anti-German *Tennessean*, tried unsuccessfully to have Edward B. Stahlman, publisher of the *Banner*, deported on the false charge of being an enemy agent. Ed Potter Jr., who founded Nashville's German-American Bank in 1916, at age nineteen, had to change the bank's name to Farmers and Merchants Bank, later Commerce Union Bank. The German Methodist Church was forced to change its name to Barth Memorial Methodist Church. Some Germantown families changed their names to avoid anti-German discrimination.

One of the many successful German-Americans in Germantown was Jacob Schnell, a grain dealer who lived with his wife, one son, and three daughters above his store on Jefferson Street. With his daughters nearing the ages when suitors should be coming by to call, Schnell built a spacious two-story house at 1111 Sixteenth Avenue South, which, early in the twentieth century, was in a fashionable neighbor-hood. When the house was finished, Mr. Schnell decided to have an elaborate party in his third-floor ballroom to introduce his daughters to Nashville society. His wife sent out engraved invitations. An orches-tra was secured, and food and flowers were ordered.

Jacob's timing was wrong as America was in a war with Germany, and Nashvillians were suspicious of anyone of German descent. Very few came to the party and certainly no one in Nashville's upper crust showed up. Schnell was furious that his daughters had been snubbed in such an uncaring way. He told his wife that their expensive mansion in one of the city's affluent neighborhoods would be allowed to fall in a state of disrepair. It would remind anyone who passed by of the injustice done his family.

Mr. Schnell moved back to Jefferson Street leaving his wife, one son, and three daughters in the grand house. His son, later a city councilman, left. One daughter married and moved away. The other two daughters, Bertha and Lena, stayed with their mother. None of them paid any attention to maintenance problems. In cold weather, pipes froze and were left unrepaired. To deal with the ensuing leaks,

Confirmation class at German Methodist Church, north Nashville, 1904   *North Nashville and Germantown*

the girls put buckets around the house to catch the water. The house was never painted and handsome draperies were allowed to rot and fall. Pigeons even got inside.

After Mrs. Schnell and Lena died, Bertha, who was well-educated and considered to be a gentle person by her few friends, retreated with her dog, Andy, into a bedroom that had no heat. She seldom came out. When neighbors brought her water and food, they were horrified to find her wearing rags.

Bertha died June 30, 1974, still in her house. She was eighty-four years old. Some rat-infested furnishings were sold at auction and everything else disappeared. The house was demolished in 1982. Thus, a sad story finally had closure. Today, the High Five Building stands on the site.

World War II

My Remembrances of World War II

The Contributor 6/19/2021

I learned of the Japanese attack on Pearl Harbor on December 7, 1941, when I was visiting my grandmother Wills at her home "Far Hills" [now the Governor's Mansion] on Curtiswood Lane in Nashville. We heard the attack announced over WSM on a cold Sunday afternoon. My parents, my brother and sister, an aunt and uncle, and three first cousins, along with my grandmother, were mostly gathered in the sitting room where we usually congregated after Sunday family dinner. I was six years old at the time.

I specifically recall the excited reaction of Senter Crook, who was my aunt Mamie Craig's husband. He had an inboard motor boat docked at a marina on the Cumberland River near Nashville. Senter loved his boat and illogically thought it might be in some danger. I recall him saying that he better get over there and make sure it was okay.

I remember taking part in war-related scrap paper drives that were organized by Parmer School, on Leake Avenue, which I attended from 1940 until 1948. Sometime after the Army's General Medical and Surgical Hospital, called Thayer, was established on White Bridge Road, Mr. O'Brien, a grandfather of my best friend, Jimmy Meadows, was employed there as a security guard. As Mr. O'Brien lived with the

Meadows a few houses down the street from my home, I often talked with him about his victory garden, the war, and the German prisoners who were convalescing at the hospital.

German prisoners were still at Thayer Hospital in the fall of 1945 when I was an almost never used 6th-grade substitute on the Parmer School football team. The Germans wore white bathrobes and pajamas as they sat in the bleachers or stood along the sidelines and watched us play.

I also remember seeing minesweepers being built and launched at the Nashville Bridge Company on the Cumberland River, across from downtown, and recall being proud that ocean-going Naval ships were being made in my hometown 1,300 miles from the sea and that fighter planes were also being made at Nashville's Vultee plant.

I recall that we had a victory garden in our back lot where my father hybridized iris. I also remember that my parents bought war savings bonds for themselves and for me and my brother and sister. The song which sometimes came to mind during the war started with the words "Over There, Over There . . ." It was a World War I song which we played and heard during World War II. I also remember playing for hours with a metal toy soldier collection which I prized. We also had a map of the world into which my father stuck pins to show the progress of the war in both theaters. Later, an older friend in the army brought home a Japanese bayonet which was of great interest to me and the other kids in the neighborhood. One of my first cousins used it to impersonate a Japanese officer. Inadvertently, he stuck himself in the thigh with it, causing considerable bleeding but no serious damage except to his pride.

I was aware of the existence of the Air Force Classification Center on Thompson Lane near the L&N Railroad overpass. I also knew a little about military activities at Seward Air Force Base in Smyrna, at Fort Campbell, and at Camp Forest, outside Tullahoma.

On weekends during World War II, Nashville was flooded with soldiers and airmen from these installations. They seemed to be everywhere—sleeping in the main waiting room at Union Station, waiting at the Greyhound Bus Terminal on Commerce Street, at the YMCA

Red Cross volunteers serve World War II soldiers coffee in Union Station
Collection of Ridley Wills II

which provided all sorts of services for them, including dances on Saturday nights) and at the First Presbyterian Church on weekends, where they were fed and where they spent nights on cots in Fellowship Hall and in our Sunday School Building.

For several summers during the war, I rode the Tennessee Central and Southern railroads in the company of my older brother and soldiers, on my way to camp. We were headed to Asheville, North Carolina, where we were met by a van which took Matt and me and other campers to Camp Sequoyah near Weaverville, North Carolina. I recall sitting up with the soldiers all night on the train because pullman berths were difficult to obtain. I also remember celebrating at Camp Sequoyah when the word came that the war was over.

I also remember gasoline rationing. It seems to me that my parents were given cards or script which entitled them to buy limited amounts of gasoline. Years later, I heard that when a Vanderbilt intern married during the war, he collected all the gasoline cards he could so that he and his bride could drive all the way to Cumberland State

Park for their honeymoon. They ran out of gas in Sparta coming back to Nashville.

I recall that John K. Maddin, who was married to my mother's sister, Elizabeth, was a member of the Civil Air Patrol during World War II. I was impressed that he had an aviation map of the United States on the wall of his library. The map showed airline distances between airports and the location of beacons and other information of interest to aviators and air controllers. I also recall that citizens, children and adults, were encouraged to memorize the silhouettes of friendly and enemy aircraft so that we could identify the latter should Nashville be attacked. We had a beacon on the top of the highest hill in Percy Warner Park. I would hold my breath so as not to take a breath until it completed its 360-degree sweep.

The Joe Werthan Servicemen's Center was established during the war by Joe Werthan, of Werthan Bag Company. It was located on Elliston Place just north of Father Ryan High School. All enlisted men were invited to spend nights there without cost.

On Saturdays, I nearly always attended the Happiness Club at the Belle Meade Theater. There, before the feature, usually a Western, came on the screen, we watched the war news, which often seemed to consist of watching German soldiers goose-stepping down a street in Warsaw or somewhere else in Europe.

I looked on President Roosevelt as a hero; I remember that he was often at Warm Springs, Georgia, because of his polio, and distinctly recall that I was walking down the middle of Belle Meade Boulevard, looking for street railroad spikes (the streetcar line had been abandoned a few years earlier), when I heard someone shout from a car that President Roosevelt had died. As I was only eleven years old when the war ended and as no members of my immediate family were active in the war much less killed, I don't think it significantly influenced my life. As a young boy, I looked upon it more with fascination than with horror.

Epilogue

Not only is Ridley Wills the author of this collection of historical remembrances, he is also my father. He has been a historian for my entire adult life. When I was in middle school, I can recall him leaving a multigenerational family career in the insurance business to become a historian. Since then, he has written and published thirty books on local history. I have often recounted that his example of choosing to follow a life of research and writing about his hometown community has given me license to follow the path which led me to becoming a cofounder of *The Contributor*.

We also share a lifelong love for the ministries of the Downtown Presbyterian Church, where this 1914 quote from Rev. James I. Vance is enshrined:

> Give me a church where life is densest, and human
> need is greatest—not a church in some sequestered
> sylvan retreat, not a temple in some lonely solitude
> far removed from the walks of life and attended only
> by the children of privilege and leisure, but give me
> a church whose doorstep is on the pavement, against
> whose walls beat and lap the tides of labor, whose
> hymns mingle with the rattle of cars and the groans
> of traffic, whose seats are within easy reach of men
> falling under heavy burdens, and whose altars are
> hallowed by the publican's prayer.

This church resides in the historic, Egyptian Revival building featured on the cover of this book and is the home of *The Contributor*.

On top of offering his "Nashville History Corner" articles, Ridley Wills has offered sage advice and financial support for the operations of *The Contributor*. His experience in the non-profit community, serving as board chairs for the YMCA of Middle TN, the Cumberland Museum and Science Center, the United Way, and Montgomery Bell Academy, to name a few, proved incalculable in giving advice and amplifying the voice and cause of *The Contributor* vendors and other writers in helping us fundraise. His articles alone though have held the attention of Nashvillians of all stripes. Readers have written to offer to take my father on trips to historical sites that he has written about. And, in a meeting with former Nashville Mayor Bill Purcell, the ex-mayor said he bought *The Contributor* to read the "Nashville History Corner" because it always taught him something he didn't know.

— *Tom Wills*

References in Captions

Art Work of Nashville 1894 and 1901, reproduction sponsored by Tennessee Historical Society (a Whipporwill Publication).

John Lawrence Connelly, ed., *North Nashville and Germantown: Yesterday and Today* (North High Association, Inc., 1982), photos insert.

Margaret Brown Coppinger, Herschel Gower, Samuel H. Howell, and Georgianna D. Overby, *Beersheba Springs: A History* (Beersheba Springs Historical Society, 1983).

Wilbur Foster Creighton, *Building of Nashville*, revised by Wilbur F. Creighton Jr. and Leland R. Johnson (copyright © 1969, Wilbur F. Creighton Jr. and Elizabeth Creighton Schumann), 51.

Jan Duke, text and captions, *Historic Photos of Nashville* (Nashville: Turner Publishing, 2005), 116.

Walter T. Durham and James W. Thomas, *A Pictorial History of Sumner County, Tennessee, 1786–1986* (Gallatin, TN: Sumner County Historical Society in cooperation with First and National Bank, 1986), 42.

John Egerton, *Nashville: The Faces of Two Centuries, 1780–1980* (Plus-Media, 1979).

James A. Hoobler, *Cities Under the Gun: Images of Occupied Nashville and Chattanooga* (Nashville: Rutledge Hill Press, 1986), 100.

Herman Justi, ed., *The Official History of the Tennessee Centennial Exposition, Nashville 1897* (published under the direction of Dr. W. L. Dudley and G. H. Baskette of the Committee on Publication), frontispiece, 81, 207.

Rudolph Kampmeier, *Recollections, the Department of Medicine, Vanderbilt University School of Medicine, 1925–1959* (Nashville: Vanderbilt University Press, 1980).

Vance Little, *Historic Brentwood*, photographs by Doug Brachey (JM Productions, 1985).

Fred Russell and Maxwell E. Benson, *Fifty Years of Vanderbilt Football* (Nashville: 1938).

Capt. Eric William Sheppard, *Bedford Forrest, the Confederacy's Greatest Cavalryman* (New York: Dial Press, 1930), frontispiece.

Charlotte A. Williams, *The Centennial Club of Nashville: A History from 1905–77* (1978).

T. Harry Williams, *Huey Long, a Biography* (New York: Alfred A. Knopf, 1969), photos insert.